the first drop of rain

Resources by Les and Leslie Parrott

Also by Leslie Parrott
If You Ever Needed Friends, It's Now
You Matter More Than You Think
God Loves You Nose to Toes (children's book)
Marshmallow Clouds (children's book)

Books
Becoming Soul Mates
The Complete Guide to Marriage Mentoring
Getting Ready for the Wedding
I Love You More (and workbooks)
Just the Two of Us
Love Is . . .
The Love List
Love Talk (and workbooks)
Meditations on Proverbs for Couples
The Parent You Want to Be
Pillow Talk
Questions Couples Ask
Relationships (and workbook)
Saving Your Marriage Before It Starts (and workbooks)
Saving Your Second Marriage Before It Starts (and workbooks)
3 Seconds
51 Creative Ideas for Marriage Mentors
Trading Places (and workbooks)
Your Time-Starved Marriage (and workbooks)

Video Curriculum — ZondervanGroupware®
Complete Resource Kit for Marriage Mentoring
I Love You More
Love Talk
Saving Your Marriage Before It Starts

Audio
I Love You More
Love Talk
Saving Your Marriage Before It Starts
Saving Your Second Marriage Before It Starts
The Parent You Want to Be
Trading Places
When Bad Things Happen to Good Marriages
You Matter More Than You Think
Your Time-Starved Marriage

the first drop
of rain

leslie parrott

ZONDERVAN®

ZONDERVAN.com/
AUTHORTRACKER
follow your favorite authors

002000262392

ZONDERVAN

The First Drop of Rain
Copyright © 2009 by The Foundation for Healthy Relationships

This title is also available as a Zondervan ebook. Visit www.zondervan.com/ebooks.

This title is also available in a Zondervan audio edition. Visit www.zondervan.fm.

Requests for information should be addressed to:

Zondervan, *Grand Rapids, Michigan 49530*

Library of Congress Cataloging-in-Publication Data

Parrott, Leslie L., 1964–
    The first drop of rain / Leslie Parrott.
       p. cm.
    ISBN 978-0-310-27248-9 (hardcover)
    1. Consolation. 2. Suffering—Religious aspects—Christianity.
  3. Encouragement—Religious aspects—Christianity. I. Title.
    BV4905.3.P37 2009
    248.8'6—dc22   2009000090

Published in association with Yates & Yates, www.yates2.com.

Interior design by Beth Shagene

Printed in the United States of America

09 10 11 12 13 14 • 23 22 21 20 19 18 17 16 15 14 13 12 11 10 9 8 7 6 5 4 3 2 1

For Ophelia's daughters with much love
Adrianne, Marilyn, Kay, and Jill

Contents

part iii

part iv

a note to the reader

As I have written these pages from my rainy corner of the world, I have felt the warm companionship of you, my reader, and a deep gratitude for the investment you are making in your own life, your own relationships, and your own work and call.

As you read this book, I want you to feel free to approach it in your own way, at your own pace.

For some of you, that might mean taking the book as a whole, stopping occasionally to write your own thoughts as you ponder the questions. You may want to do some journaling as you engage with the content and poetry that comes from the pages of my own personal journals.

If you tend toward the contemplative side, you may prefer taking a more devotional approach to the book. You might read just one of the brief chapters each day, mindfully pondering the questions that are contained within.

Still others might find that each of the four parts is ideal for a four-session small group study. Your small group or book club can use the questions at the end of each chapter as discussion starters to guide and deepen your shared learning experience.

More than anything, I hope you will find your own way through these pages, and more than that, through any dry and fragile moments, hours or days, I hope you will find your way to the miracle of that first drop of rain.

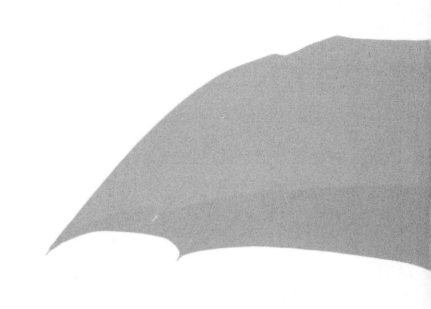

part i

seattle rain

Here in Seattle we think a lot about rain. Actually I don't need to *think* much about rain — I never carry an umbrella and rarely pull on a coat — but rain is an ever-present part of the landscape, my reality. It's a steady companion, a gentle mist that follows me, day by damp day.

Rain, with its dark skies, gray days, and dreariness, is liquid disappointment. Rain is a symbol of ruin, a catalyst for corrosion, a creator of rust. We steel ourselves, stockpiling resources for a rainy day. Discouragement dampens our spirit, and no one likes to hang around a wet blanket. Rain is a pain, a bother. Our children sing, "Rain, rain, go away, come again some other day."

Yet this is not the whole story. In the forty-fifth year of my rain-drenched life, I have come to see rain as compelling proof of God's gracious, giving nature.

An absence of rain turns a place into a desert, a wasteland. If you've ever been parched and felt faint and studied the horizon for the smallest sign of hope, then you know the feeling. You know the feeling of hope at a softly darkening sky, the sharp-sweet scent of wet air, and the transparent but tangible first drop of rain.

That first drop of rain begins a transformation from hunger to fruitfulness. Rain streams down from clouds like banners across the landscape of your life.

The rain in Seattle is soft today, something between a drizzle and a mist. It's not showoff rain like the magnificent storms from my childhood in Kansas. It's a continuous slick soundtrack to my life. Most days it's so familiar that it fades into the background. It's not until I find a still, introspective center that I am captivated by the rain. My eyes follow drops outside the leaded window, drops that sparkle and shine as they form, fall, slide, and gather in shifting, mirrored pools. Each drop holds eternity — from cloud to ground and back, world without end.

A professor once told me that nothing can belong to us, even our own experience, unless we understand it. I watch my life with my eyes. I touch it with my fingers. My mind considers and my heart longs. Across the landscape of my interior, truth coalesces and I begin to understand. As I write my stories, I begin to understand.

Each drop of rain is ancient and new. "If there is magic on this planet," says Loren Eisley, "it is contained in water" (*The Immense Journey*, 1957). Rain is the mystery of God's presence and God's absence across the landscape of my life.

 **to ponder**

1. What comes to your mind when you hear the word *rain*? Is it positive or negative and why?

2. When you hear that nothing can belong to us, even our own experience, unless we understand it, what do you think? Do you agree? Why or why not?

the wasteland

What are the roots that clutch, what branches grow
Out of this stony rubbish? Son of man,
You cannot say, or guess, for you know only
A heap of broken images, where the sun beats.

T. S. Eliot

All too often I find myself in the desert of life, peering up at the beating sun in a cloudless sky. This is the wasteland. T. S. Eliot's *The Waste Land* describes this desert life. I first encountered Eliot's visionary poem as an undergraduate when I signed up for a required literature course. As it happened, the course — focused entirely on *The Waste Land* — changed my life. As my professor helped us see the layers of allusion, language, and imagery, I felt my spirit expanding. It was the deepest encounter I had ever had with the printed word outside the Bible.

I became a student of poetry and of culture. The course opened my eyes to how much there is to know and say. I saw layers beyond the surface. I understood that something true in its simplest form grows truer still as you unpack the wisdom within. *The Waste Land* contains narrative from Scripture — Ezekiel, Isaiah, Ecclesiastes, Psalms, Philippians, the Gospels — and is replete with images borrowed from and allusions to the great works of Milton, Chaucer, Shakespeare, Whitman, and Dante. Eliot weaves images from great operas, celebrated plays, and masterful visual art. The English language cannot contain the poem, and it spills over to include Greek and Sanskrit. *The Waste Land* is a difficult delight.

Studying this poem taught me how to be thoughtful about my own experiences. It taught me that image and metaphor can reach my heart, that insight is gained more easily through indirect teaching. When we allow ourselves to be caught up in a story that isn't ours, our guard drops and, almost without realizing it, we are able to draw conclusions that are both personal and insightful.

Eliot makes visible the unseen journey of life and faith. His poem, even twenty-five years after I first read it, describes my interior landscape with startling accuracy. It helped to form my understanding of how vast, complex, and layered the territory of the soul is — a great stretch of undiscovered wasteland.

Now I am forty-five and balancing the parenting of two young boys — spelling tests, book reports, Sunday school, soccer games, ortho appointments, vision therapy, field trips, play dates, and something important I'm forgetting — with a marriage of nearly twenty-four years and a career that requires frequent travel and weekly teaching responsibilities. And still, Eliot's words nurture me. On my way home from work with the never-ending skritch-sloosh of the windshield wipers, Eliot's lines come to mind: "At the violet hour, when the eyes and back / turn upward from the desk / when the human engine waits."

I watch the sky turn to deeper hues of blue violet and finally darken. That transformation pulls me away from urgent details of my daily life into a hushed reverence, into the quietness of God's presence in the darkening sky.

When my life is a desert, I feel dry enough to crumble into a handful of dust. Like this morning. I set my alarm for 5:45 to steal a bit of time for coffee and contemplation, for a momentary echo of the interior conversations I used to engage in before kids and chaos intervened. I sport granny glasses now — not because I need them but because I am so tired my eyes won't focus (maybe I do need them the teensiest bit). Glasses perched, I sip my coffee, spiked with French vanilla cream, and attempt to focus on my Bible, on what God is doing here and now and how I am to cooperate.

Life seems as blurry and unreadable as the small print. Like when three of my dear friends told me they are moving across the country simultaneously. When a recent phone call told me my aunt — between jobs and without health insurance — woke in the middle of the night with a feverish illness. When my son's emotional meltdowns must mean *something* important that I can't manage to discern.

I don't need to know every answer. I just need, for a moment, to get my head above these present circumstances. What is God revealing to me? Where is he moving? What is my place in this world?

But what I *really* want as I sip my coffee is to go back to sleep. That's when my son Jackson runs out of the bedroom to snuggle with me on the couch. I look at the clock. We have thirty minutes to get out the door before my other son, John, gets a tardy slip. I hurry through the required motions — not with deep inner strength and certitude, but with puffy eyes, blurry vision, and anxiety about how I'll navigate the day ahead.

This is where I live — somewhere between the wasteland and the rain.

 to ponder

1. When do you most feel like you are traveling in the desert of life? Be specific. What makes you feel this way?

2. Do you ever feel as if you are living between the wasteland and the rain? Why?

Rain

You coalesce in clouds
Grow heavy
Stretch
Let go
Snap into a tiny ball
And fall
Gathering speed in flight
Liquid simplicity
Transparent as glass
Yet holding mysteries beyond
Our knowing
Locked in molecules and gas.
How is it you defy gravity?
Drawing nutrients up
To nurture plants,
And more amazing still,
Throughout me.
You act as a prism — reflecting light
Creating rainbows in your flight.

Dissolving rocks
You trickle down
And at the lowest point
Begin to rise
Changed by the sun
(A new disguise)
Until you find your home
With other drops
A cloud to form.
I stand
And let you drench me down
I see your pools
Collecting on the ground
But all the while I sense
Hinting at Something
You are a clue
A reflection
Of the One
Who is not you.

seeing double

I could not
Speak, and my eyes failed, I was neither
Living nor dead, and I knew nothing,
Looking into the heart of light, the silence.

T. S. Eliot

My spiritual vision is declining in clarity as rapidly as my eyes. When I was younger, I expected that by now I'd finally have my act together. This idealized spiritual me wouldn't have to grope in the dark anymore. Nope, my body might fade, but my spiritual vision would get better every year.

What never occurred to me was that my spiritual growth might involve a *decline* in my spiritual optics. At a time in my life when I expected to be spiritually capable and confident, I am straining and squinting. Life is blurry. Without the vision of the Spirit, I'm blind as a bat and I'm no longer too proud to admit it.

My son Jackson was recently diagnosed with a vision problem. His eyes weren't working together, so to prevent him from seeing double, his brain shut down the sight in one eye. During the eye test, the optometrist covered Jackson's strong eye and held up pictures for him to describe. They were right in front of his face, yet he could not see them. Fortunately, with glasses and vision therapy, this can be corrected.

Our brains are hardwired to protect us from the confusion of seeing double. It is quite possible to become blind even while we are physically capable of sight.

Blindness is a common subject in the Bible and with Jesus: "These are people — whose eyes are open but don't see a thing" (Mark 4:12). In my circle of close friends, I love it when someone challenges me with "Leslie, when did you get blind?" They love me enough to speak the truth. I need to correct my vision. Here I am in midlife, echoing the cry of the blind beggars who cried out to Jesus, "Have mercy on me!" More than ever, I know this: I can't live without corrected vision.

 to ponder

1. Do you ever feel like life is blurry? Do you feel as if you are straining and squinting for spiritual clarity and sight? When are you most likely to experience this "blindness"?

2. Have you ever experienced the grace of "corrected" spiritual vision? What insights did you gain?

broken images

A heap of broken images, where the sun beats,
And the dead tree gives no shelter, the cricket no relief,
And the dry stone no sound of water.

T. S. Eliot

My dear friend Kathy is a delicious combination of articulate and obstinate — she once misspoke her own birth date and then proceeded to defend her error with such passion and principle that I half expected her birth certificate to change.

Kathy and Kevin, her husband of eighteen years, live with their daughter, Meg, in Kansas. Friends for decades, our families have become vacation buddies — over the years we've traveled to several countries and what feels like most US cities. We've hiked jagged glaciers in Alaska, sipped cappuccino in Paris, gone swimming in the warm turquoise waters of Baja, California, and shivered through odorous cheese factories. We like doing almost anything, and we love doing it together.

On our last visit, at our home in Seattle, Kathy had a low-grade fever and the same persistent cough she'd had the last two or three times we'd been together. Six weeks later came the diagnosis: lung cancer, small cell. Kathy, my health-conscious, non-smoking, active friend had cancer. It was unreal.

Every day since, Kathy has been locked in the fight of her life. She interviewed doctors, settling on the most aggressive specialist whose passionate commitment to battle cancer gave him a colorful vocabulary. Somehow, it seemed appropriate to have him curse her cancer — talking to it like the enemy it is.

What do you think when someone who has poured her life into blessing others now feels the fire of poison poured into her own veins? How can you pray when cancer begins to take the life of the person who always prayed for you?

When I could no longer endure physical separation from my friend, I finagled an open window in my schedule and a miraculous last-minute flight to Kansas. I landed in the kind of storm we rarely get in Seattle — an electric storm, rising water, power outages. Kathy was in the hospital. It was the day before her birthday. Three months had passed since we'd touched; her skin was translucent and tight and her healthy frame was skeletal. Long blonde hair had fallen out. Radiation had burned her esophagus, making talking and eating excruciating.

> *The soul would have no rainbow had the eyes no tears.*
> **John Vance Cheney**

I sat beside Kathy's bed that night. Outside, lightning flashed and sheets of water spread across the dark city. Wanting to protect Kathy's searing throat from further injury, I struggled to carry on a one-sided conversation. I somehow felt I could hold off her suffering by creating a wall of words that would be a hedge of protection around Kathy's thoughts, filling them with amusing anecdotes and updates. I followed my stream of consciousness down every tributary, chattering on about things. Like the time my friend Bonnie, who had spent ten minutes looking for her lost cell phone in her car (while talking to me on that very cell phone) until it dawned on her what she was doing and she sheepishly told me she'd been utterly distracted as we chatted by the serious search for her phone.

Kathy smiled, fueling my chatter. There was nothing I could say that was important enough for this moment, and yet somehow everything I said was made important by this moment, no matter how incidental and inane. All that mattered was our proximity: Kathy supported by her angled hospital bed, my body draped sideways over the visitor chair so I could slide up closer beside her.

On the flight home, I scrawled this poem on a paper napkin. Hot tears rolled down my cheeks as images tumbled onto paper. As soon as the plane landed, I called Kathy and read it to her, the lump in my throat pressing hard against the words.

For Kathy

It didn't rain, it poured
Flashes of lightning,
Power outages
We watched the creek rise
But you were all
I could see or feel —
Your cancer was the real storm
We were all brave
Telling stories
And you let me rub
Your fuzzy "Velcro" head
We turned on the TV
For tornado warnings
But it was the blood draw results
That made our news
White cells in the decimals.
We washed, pulled on our masks and gloves
Not wanting our very presence
To become another threat.
We hung a bright banner
Opened little gifts —
Tomorrow would be the dawn
Of a new year for you.
I didn't make a birthday wish
I prayed,

God give her grace
Pour health into her body
And soul
Dissolve fear
Give us reason to celebrate.
On the flight home I see you there
Determined (or is it defiant)
Enough
To down hospital scrambled eggs,
Oatmeal with no brown sugar
And meatloaf.
It hits me
You've re-defined everything
As in "If Kathy
(Who can't so much as order eggs
in a restaurant because she can't stand them)
Can eat hospital eggs
With a burned throat
in searing pain,
then surely I can . . ."
My eyes fill with tears
mostly of joy.
I didn't know I could love you more
but now I do.

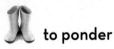 **to ponder**

1. Have you ever experienced a time when life felt like "a heap of broken images, where the sun beats"? What was that experience like for you?

2. When have you been a traveling companion for someone walking through their own wasteland? How did it change you?

relentless sun

Burning burning burning burning
O Lord Thou pluckest me out
O Lord Thou pluckest.

T. S. Eliot

These are the moments when what is most real is unseen. The desert of the soul and the unbearable heat. This is life beneath the relentless sun of suffering.

Have you ever felt plucked and dropped by the hand of God into the burning? Where is your desert place? Do you feel desolate, dry, and fragile? Is the sun beating on the broken images of your dreams? Is there no sign of God, no sound of water?

We keep walking even when the journey isn't one we planned. My friend Kathy's way of traveling her cancer journey is to be reverent about the things that matter, irreverent about what doesn't, and wise enough to know the difference.

Yet it doesn't make the trip any easier. The shadow of a rocky landscape darkened Kathy's eyes. There was real fear and grief; there was deep physical suffering. The constant pain of cancer and chemo left her utterly depleted. Dehydrated, malnourished, and severely sleep deprived, Kathy was in the hospital again.

The well-meaning words of a visiting doctor sounded like a death sentence to Kathy. The doctor was sympathetic — too sympathetic. The weight pressed down. Fear grew into panic. She felt her life becoming nothing more than statistics and pessimistic predictions.

Kathy couldn't sleep. Her normal brain function began to fail. Too many days with too little rest had left her with no resources. Her fear intensified, like a song playing over and over in her mind. Darkness closed in. Depression had a stranglehold.

> *If it can be verified, we don't need faith.... Faith is for that which lies on the other side of reason. Faith is what makes life bearable with all its tragedies and ambiguities and sudden, startling joys.*
>
> **Madeline L'Engle**

Kevin calls us in Seattle to invite us to support Kathy in this dark night. We begin to pray. In Kansas, Kathy's mother-in-law and sister-in-law lock hands around her hospital bed and pray for release from fear. They pray for rest. In Washington, we do the same.

Kathy remembers her eyes growing strangely heavy before she drifted off to sleep, awash in peace. When she woke up, the cancer was still there, along with the pain. But the restful sleep had been real. Walking through the wasteland, she had found a sliver of shade, tasted a drop of cool rain.

 to ponder

1. When have the words or actions of a well-meaning "helper" been damaging to your spirit? Were you able to recover and forgive? If so, how did you do this? If not, can you now consider forgiving that person?

2. Have you ever had the experience of unexplainable peace or rest in the midst of personal suffering? How did that occur for you?

unreal city

Unreal City,
Under the brown fog of a winter dawn,
A crowd flowed over London Bridge, so many.

T. S. Eliot

Seattle is a city of distinct neighborhoods that perch on wooded hillsides. Magnolia is manicured, Phinney Ridge is funky, Capitol Hill is edgy, and Queen Anne Hill — my neighborhood for over fifteen years — is cozy. A. J. Meat Market has been providing fresh Thanksgiving turkeys for over fifty years; The 5 Spot serves a delectable spinach and mushroom scramble; Macrina's Bakery makes the best brown sugar shortbread cookies I've ever tasted; and I know the clerk at the grocery store. I love the neighborhood.

So when we made the surprising choice to leave our cozy home nestled on a cul-de-sac for an apartment in the heart of downtown Seattle, our friends figured we were either bold or dumb. Our new place is just four blocks from the Space Needle, on the seventeenth floor of a high-rise, and it has a Starbucks in the lobby. Still, why did we choose to leave such a wonderful neighborhood for an unknown one?

I can't explain why. I only know that we needed to move. We felt drawn, if not called, to center our family in the soul of Seattle.

And we have. There is so much about it that is inherently good. After dinner we walk to Lake Union, where an old fishing vessel has become a "pirate" ship in the imagination of our boys. We gaze at colossal dinosaur fossils at the Science Center just four blocks away. My son John had his birthday party aboard the monorail and devoured the world-famous "Lunar Orbiter" dessert atop the Space Needle. The city is a place of endless adventures.

But the city is not always a place of light. One of the dark places that our family cares about is the park across the street from our condo. Denny Park, Seattle's oldest public park, is a welcome patch of green amid the towers of glass and cement. Overgrown trees and gigantic rhododendron run rampant. Patches of grass look fresh and inviting. Our boys imagine a zip-line straight from our deck to the heart of the park.

But Denny Park has another side. It's not unusual to find used needles or to catch a glimpse of an exchange. I have seen a woman behind a flowering rhododendron jab a syringe into the back of her knee. The cool shade of the park becomes cold shadows. The things that lurk in those shadows scare me.

> And when it rains on your parade, look up rather than down. Without the rain, there would be no rainbow.
>
> **G. K. Chesterton**

One hot summer day, while sitting in the park watching my boys play, my thoughts turned toward Jonah and how God called him to the city of Nineveh. Jonah tried his best to ignore this call and keep his safe suburban life, far from such an obviously wild city. But safety wasn't what God was calling Jonah to.

It is amazing that God was so personal with Jonah — one solitary man — and at the same time with the whole city of Nineveh. We all know the story — the storm, sailors casting lots, the whale, and, finally, the obedience. But then comes the time afterward.

Jonah sits in the desert, shaded by a single plant, to await the destruction of Nineveh, when God's judgment fire will rain down and wipe the city out with apocalyptic drama. Thankfully, his wait was in vain.

 **to ponder**

1. Have you ever felt called to something totally unexpected? Do you feel a nudge at this time toward transition into a new call? Describe what you are feeling.

2. When have you been challenged to move out of your comfort zone and into a new context? Remember what that was like.

beneath the shadow

I will show you something different from either
Your shadow at morning striding behind you
Or your shadow at evening rising to meet you;
I will show you fear in a handful of dust.

T. S. Eliot

A few of us formed a group called "Friends of Denny Park." Linked by nothing more than a passion for Seattle and this park, we gather, often in my apartment, to collaborate on vision, strategy, and funding to restore the beauty of our park and renew its ability to serve as a safe space of shade and play. Our circle includes a representative from the parks and recreation department, a graduate student pursuing city planning, an urban architect, area merchants (including the owner of an "organic" vodka bar), a journalist, an advocate for homeless adults who need safe public spaces, and neighbors who care.

We gather over coffee (sometimes donated by Starbucks) with our clean pads of paper, and we brainstorm. Who should we involve? How can we drum up funding? What might the park become? We make presentations to urban alliances and neighborhood groups. We organize volunteers from nearby churches and schools. We hold workshops in low-income city housing to hear what the children most want in a play park. We canvass the neighborhood and pass out brochures. We've won a few grants from the City Council and the Department of Neighborhoods and enlisted the support of our local Starbucks and a major Seattle developer. We are planning the inaugural Block Party in the Park, with musicians, artists, merchants, and locals. In this city of rain, we long to see this wasteland begin to grow again.

Meteorologists tell us that cities can literally create rain; clouds form more quickly in the heated air. The features of the urban wasteland — cars, concrete, factories, and fumes — are catalysts for life-giving rain.

> *It ain't no use putting up your umbrella till it rains.*
> **Alice Caldwell Rice**

In the same way, cities call forth the presence of God. The heat of longing, secrecy, and sin rises like prayers to the heart of God, and God's presence rains down in showers and storms of grace. Maybe that's why I'm here, in this place so close to Denny Park. I want to get my hands wet — I want to see the storm up close.

 ## to ponder

1. Have you ever pursued a call that opened doors to unlikely relationships or partnerships? If so, how did that enrich your life?

2. Are there any "shadowy" places in your sphere that you would like to impact with light? What is one thing you can do to make a difference?

part ii

waiting for rain

April is the cruellest month, breeding
Lilacs out of the dead land, mixing
Memory and desire, stirring
Dull roots with spring rain.

T. S. Eliot

Just a two-and-a-half-hour ferry ride from Seattle is the Canadian island of Victoria. Part of British Columbia, Victoria is a busy tourist destination with its royal culture, formal buildings, high teas, and especially the world-renowned Butchart Gardens. Over a century old, these stunning gardens wend their way through the dips and rises of a massive abandoned quarry. There is a rose garden, a sunken garden, a Japanese garden, and an Italian garden. Butchart Gardens is a delight for any flower lover, but for my aunt Jill — whose connection to God's creative character through gardening is deep — they are a dream. And I could not resist the chance to make her dream come true.

It was mid-July. We boarded the *Victoria Clipper* at 6:30 in the morning, passports in hand — my mom, Aunt Jill (Mom's sister), and I. The weather in the Pacific Northwest is usually temperate and rainy, but Seattle had been experiencing record-breaking temperatures in the 90s. We looked forward to cool breezes and milder temperatures in Victoria, even some soothing rain.

But Victoria is located in a rain shadow. The rest of Victoria Island may have been cool and wet, but Victoria was nearly 100 degrees and sunny. We soldiered on, undeterred, despite my mother's back brace and my aunt's injured knee. In every available space, flowers bloomed, wilted but willing beneath the beating sun. While the rest of the island receives nearly 200 inches of rain annually, the rain shadow created by the Cascade Mountains reduces rainfall in Victoria to about a tenth of that.

We had high tea in the old Butchart home. Maybe it was the tea, infused with rose petals and blue buttons and berries, that inspired us, or perhaps it was the experience of being transported into another country to what seemed like another century, but our conversation turned to stories from the past — and death.

My grandmother Ophelia lost two little girls before the birth of my mom. The first little girl, Adrianne, died soon after birth because the doctor's forceps had inflicted severe brain damage. My grandmother, a pastor's wife already married for a year at the age of seventeen, had to endure this sorrow far from her family (she in Indiana, they in Texas). The

If there were the sound of water only
Not the cicada
And dry grass singing
But sound of water over a rock
Where the hermit-thrush sings in the pine trees
Drip drop drip drop drop drop drop
But there is no water.

T. S. Eliot

second death was a new kind of sorrow. Little Marilyn was about eight months old when she became sick. The doctor shrugged, said she had a simple cold. Marilyn died days later. Grandmother Ophelia was pregnant, expecting my mom, at the time of Marilyn's death.

In the Butchart tea house, we felt the weight of grief. We imagined what it must have been like for Ophelia in 1938, not yet twenty, as she awaited the birth of her third child with no confidence in the doctor and grieving in a way only the death of a child can break your heart. She seldom spoke about those days. Six years after my mom was born, she had another healthy girl, Jill. No more elaborate names. Then my grandmother was widowed at a young age and grieved again.

My grandmother, who was a teacher, had an outrageous sense of humor. She hosted spontaneous "award ceremonies" where she would give a trophy (purchased at some secondhand shop) to her "favorite" son-in-law, fostering a hilarious competition among the men in the family to find outlandish ways to please her every whim and fancy. She could raise one eyebrow at a time, instilling fear or indicating mischief, depending on the situation.

In her final days, when the past seemed more real than the present, it was her losses that rose to the surface of her memory.

I look across the table at my mother and my aunt, my grandmother's two surviving daughters, and think of the rain shadows that each of us has lived through. We each know the feeling of my grandmother's tears.

So often we begin a great adventure, expecting coolness and rain. Instead we encounter a rain shadow and the relentless heat of the sun, with no relief in sight. We scan the horizon, straining to see the first rain cloud, longing for the taste of that first drop of rain.

 **to ponder**

1. What rain shadow seasons have you lived through? Are you currently in a rain shadow? If so, what is your experience like?

2. Describe the moments when you felt the relief of that first drop of rain? How were you able to maintain hope that the rain would eventually come?

I Longed for Shade

Shade is a relief.
Cool and dark,
Shelter from the beating sun.
If there is no water
Then at least shade.
After all,
God even provided shade
To Jonah
While he waited in his wasteland.
Searching the horizon for God's burning wrath
On the reckless city.
(After the whale, the preaching, and the weeping)
Jonah, the truth is I really can relate.
I run, I hide, and sometimes
I think God's grace
Seems gentler in another place.
(God's rescues sometimes feel like getting hurled
    onto a shore.)
But back to shade,
Silhouettes can entertain,
Throwing their silent dramas on a screen.
(I'll take a diversion gladly, a moment of repose.)

But shadows,
These are different.
Darkness only — that prevents the light.
Evoking Fear —
Raising tiny hairs that line the neck.
Penumbra shadows,
More diffuse, obscuring shapes,
But filtering light.
Known objects take on vaguely familiar
But unrecognizable forms.
(My house, my favorite tree, that open door thru
    which I can't quite see)
Appearing in hospital corridors, vacant rooms,
Lonely halls and silent city streets,
Creating darkness — light retreats
Umbra shadows —
These are darker still.
Sun cannot be seen,
Like an eclipse.
I'd choose the beating sun
To this abyss.
I longed for shade —
Not ever this.

vapor rising

The awful daring of a moment's surrender
Which an age of prudence can never retract
By this, and this only, we have existed.

T. S. Eliot

The first mystery the author of Genesis explores is this: "God created the Heavens and Earth — all you see, all you don't see. Earth was a soup of nothingness, a bottomless emptiness, an inky blackness. God's Spirit brooded like a bird over the watery abyss" (Genesis 1:1 – 2).

One of the first mysteries Jesus explores is this: "Unless a person submits to this original creation — the 'wind-hovering-over-the-water' creation, the invisible moving the visible, a baptism into a new life — it's not possible to enter God's kingdom" (John 3:5). Jesus was speaking to Nicodemus, a devout Jew studying for the ministry who knew all about the creation story.

I was thinking about Nicodemus recently. We had spent the evening at the home of Rabbi Daniel Lapin and were on our way home. Rabbi Lapin and his wife, Susan, along with two of their six daughters, had invited us to join them and some of their Jewish friends for Shabbat (the Jewish Sabbath). The Lapins, while deeply rooted in their Orthodox Jewish community, are an open door of hospitality to followers of Jesus. Jewish tradition encourages hospitable community.

They live on Mercer Island in a neighborhood defined by faith. Because all labor is forbidden on Shabbat, everyone who attends synagogue must live within easy walking distance. We drove to Mercer Island from downtown Seattle and felt strangely conspicuous slamming our car doors as the other guests arrived on foot.

We gathered around the candlelit table and engaged in a ceremony of worship as we ate. There are special rituals for the washing of hands and a period of silence, followed by the breaking and blessing of the bread. Hebrew is the predominant language of worship, but our hosts graciously included English commentary. There is wine and a blessing.

During the meal, only one central conversation is cultivated; no side comments or one-on-one talking with those seated near you is allowed. I was gently scolded for drifting off into an impromptu conversation with my neighbor.

Rabbi Lapin sprinkles the meal with wise homily based on Torah readings and Jewish tradition. The meal is simultaneously scripted and spontaneous. The order and timing of the meal are disciplined, but that produces a strange freedom. Listening so intently in a group, engaging together as the Rabbi directed questions to each of us with the entire table listening in, created a higher level of conversation.

For Christians, the Shabbat is clearly the precursor to the Communion meal in which Jesus becomes our bread and wine, poured out of God's heart for our sake. The unity of the meal is the very essence of the body of Christ, deeply rooted in who God was, is, and ever will be.

Christians and Jews share the conviction that God's creative spirit shaped and is shaping our world and us. The attention and devotion to matters of the spirit during Shabbat call us to a new awareness of God's Spirit — quite a challenge in our world of busy materialism. This seems to have been the crux of Jesus' conversation with Nicodemus. There are realities of the Spirit you have become blind to, Jesus tells him. Submit again to the original "wind-hovering-over-the-water creation," a baptism into a new life.

Matters of the spirit are mysteries that dwarf us. I often find myself, like Nicodemus, procrastinating with questions, hoping to put off my moment of decision. Or worse, responding to the mystery of God's kingdom like the Israelites in the wasteland on the edge of Canaan: "a land that swallows people whole" (Numbers 13:32) and "we felt like grasshoppers" (verse 33).

My fears and flaws demand my full attention. They insist that I ignore matters of the spirit — whether past, present, or future. They maroon me in the wasteland, far from food and company — when what is available to me is a table laden with bread and wine and companions for the journey, if only I'll let myself be directed by the Wind that hovered over the water of creation. I want to see God's creative spirit brooding like a bird over the abyss of my fear, but sometimes all I can see is the inky blackness.

Pools of rainwater warmed by the sun evaporate and rise into the heavens. Jesus said it was good that he go to his Father in heaven because he would send his Spirit, the friend who would be our guide — the very Spirit of truth — to all that Jesus did and said. Like the invisible vapor rising in the air all around us, he won't draw attention to himself, but will honor Christ, giving us God's gift of himself (John 16:5 – 15).

Recently I was sitting at the front of a hotel ballroom, lined up behind a conference table with four fellow board members from our condominium association. We faced about a hundred of our neighbors engaged in a robust disagreement over our recommended increase in monthly fees. We all bought our apartments when the building was nothing but a hole in the ground with a marketing brochure promising "service as an address." For many in the room, this building was the promised land.

Just six months into our shared life in this high-rise community, there were promises unfulfilled, systems not yet working, unpleasant discoveries, and work yet to be done. An unlikely board member (I'm a mother raising my sons in the city), I felt conspicuously inadequate when the tone of the evening became adversarial. I've served on my church board and on nonprofit boards, but this was a different role. I wanted to be a good neighbor, to shape the culture of this community, and to make a difference. But on this night, as I listened to conversations about "due process," "bait and switch," and "tenant's rights clauses," I began to shut down. What did I think I had to offer? Fear overwhelmed me as I stood on the edge of a new life.

Fear feels like heat. I was cotton-mouthed, clammy, and weak. I tried to turn my attention away from the escalating dialogue in the room and toward God. What about this process is important to God? Is my role silence or speech? Is my presence significant or insignificant? God's Spirit seemed to have evaporated in the heat. I sensed that I was alone in the desert.

I snuck out. It was either that or give in to the temptation to crawl under a table and hide. I pushed through the hotel's revolving doors and out into the damp Seattle night. Three deep breaths pulled life into my constricted lungs. Around me the city hummed. People were living their particular lives, like I was living mine. Taking a final breath, I reentered the hotel and walked toward the ballroom to continue the dance.

As I reentered, I spotted my husband and two boys in the back row. They lit up when they saw me. The boys waved artwork they'd created during the meeting. They seemed untouched by the strident voices and intense proceedings. "Unless you return to square one and start over like children," said the Spirit brooding over the chaos of my life (Matthew 18:3). "This is the right road. Walk down this road" (Isaiah 30:21). I took a deep breath and walked to my seat. I listened.

The sound of rain can just barely be heard.

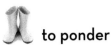 **to ponder**

1. Have you ever felt marooned in the wasteland by a preoccupation with your own flaws and fears? What specific fears demand too much of your attention? What flaws do?

2. Have you ever felt yourself procrastinating when you sense the leading of God's Spirit in your life? What action could you take now in obedient response to God?

10
chapter

what the wind is doing

My friend Arlys and I were talking. A mutual friend was in trouble, and our collective wisdom was coming up short. We mulled over some options and proposed a possible course of action. But there was a problem. That action would force us to change some much anticipated plans. We hesitated. Then Arlys, in a moment of clarity, said, "Well, I think we're supposed to be blowing in God's winds anyway."

Later I was driving through Seattle, just beyond Pike Place Market near the waterfront, and I happened to pass a looming umbrella sculpture. It stands in the middle of a street, planted on a divider between busy lanes of traffic. This red metal umbrella has been blown inside out by the wind. Set on a pivoting base, it swings in the wind, blowing in one direction and then another.

I immediately identified with it. God's winds begin to blow, and I whip out my umbrella for protection and try to resist, only to watch the umbrella be whipped inside out, rendering me vulnerable.

Mark's account of Jesus out on the stormy Sea of Galilee with his disciples is captivating. After a long day of teaching, Jesus climbs aboard the boat and falls asleep as the disciples head across the water. I know that feeling well. After a day of speaking at a conference, my adrenaline crashes like clockwork, and the sleep that follows is a deep, unnatural, groggy stupor.

Jesus seems to be a bit grumpy when the disciples wake him in the midst of an unexpected storm. Every mom knows that feeling. The kids awaken us from a moment of desperately needed slumber with an "urgent" need that seems quite incidental. Jesus speaks to the storm like a mom might speak to her unruly children: "Quiet! Settle down!" Mark tells us that "the wind ran out of breath; the sea became smooth as glass" (Mark 4:39).

> *I'm singing in the rain, just singing in the rain; What a wonderful feeling, I'm happy again.*
> **Arthur Freed**

I feel powerful when my children obey me instantly (as they do, well, *most* of the time). But Jesus has authority over both the wind and the sea, something that astonishes the disciples — and me.

I get the point — Jesus is truly in charge. So why do I still have such a hard time with the storms in my life? So often, panic seizes me. Right now, my beloved father-in-law is in the grip of illness and seems to be sinking. My husband, the youngest of three sons, his father's namesake, is drowning beneath waves of insomnia, worry, and grief.

I know God is in charge of life and death. But here in the boat, water is pouring in and the waves are building. How can I help my husband? My umbrella is inside out. I taste the rain. I feel the wind.

Lord, the sea is so wide and my boat is so small. Where will the wind blow us?

 **to ponder**

1. When have you experienced the winds of life blowing so hard it was as if your umbrella turned inside out and you had no protection?

2. Can you identify any place in your life where you are blowing in God's winds, allowing him to redirect you? What specifically do you sense God asking you to do?

Looking Up

Clouds do absolutely nothing
To call attention to themselves.
They float,
Silently, indifferently,
Contentedly
Above
White puffs against the blue
To notice them
You have to stop your motion
Be still.
Look up.
But clouds aren't still,
They drift.
Sometimes obscuring the sun
Or moon
And when something isn't clear—
When the truth is obscured from us
We say
"It's cloudy."

Clouds are collectors.
Drops of water congeal
Connected in suspension
Laced together
Hanging between heaven and earth —
Like my hammock.
Until they spill over
(My hammock spills me out too.)
The cloud disappears into rain.
Rain gets my attention.
It races to me,
Unbidden.
Touches any exposed skin,
Soaks in.
Clings.
But these days,
My head is in the clouds.

low clouds

Who is the third who walks always beside you?
When I count, there are only you and I together
But when I look ahead up the white road
There is always another one walking beside you…
—But who is that on the other side of you?

T. S. Eliot

The biggest surprise of living on the seventeenth floor is how connected we feel to the sky. There's so much to look at outside our windows — the Space Needle, Lake Union, the Cascade Mountains, the cityscape; ferries and sea planes come and go, the monorail zooms by. These are the players, but what I thought of as just the backdrop — the sky — is really the star of the show. Wisps of cotton form endless patterns, the perfect I-Spy game for little boys. By turns dark and stormy, or brimming with golden morning sunlight, or showing off brilliant sunset colors, the sky and the clouds are always alive. Sometimes the clouds wrap themselves around our high-rise, reminding me of Robert Frost's words, "The clouds are low and hairy in the skies like locks blown forward in the gleam of eyes."

If there is one thing I want more of in my life, it is clarity. I always imagined insight and clarity were the backdrop, like the clouds in the sky. And of course, I would have a sense of what is important. Of course, I would know what needs tending and what needs ignoring. Of course, I would be clear about right and wrong. Of course.

Yet, like the ever-changing whispered patterns of clouds, my fleeting thoughts shift and reconfigure. The patterns that seemed so recognizable change their shape before my next glance. I want to know, *really* know, what I should be doing in every area of my life, but I can't get a handle on it.

My boys press their faces into the windows of our apartment. As they look out at the clouds, they create their own clouds of breath that actually prevent them from seeing as clearly. Sometimes, in my eager, overanxious, too-intense desire to see life with clarity, I create my own cloud cover. Now I see through a glass darkly.

Sometimes you do your best despite the darkness. My friends Doug and Margo met a six-week-old baby girl who needed a safe, loving home, so they took her in. No formal papers, just love. The biological mom wasn't able to be the nurturing presence Jazzmyn needed. She knew that, but, periodically, in her healthiest and most stable moments, she felt the loss of her baby girl. The dad was in prison. Over time, Doug and Margo developed such a love for little Jazzmyn

> *Into each life some rain must fall.*
> **Henry Wadsworth Longfellow**

that they hoped and prayed she could belong to them. Out of deep respect for the mom's place in Jazzmyn's life, they waited for her to release Jazzmyn to them. She had chosen them and relied on them but still had a deep ambivalence about giving up her baby.

The time came when Jazzmyn's biological mother decided to allow the adoption. Doug and Margo rejoiced. But Jazzmyn's dad — in prison, guilty of serious offenses, unsafe as a dad — fought the adoption. A trial was held. Tens of thousands of dollars were spent during months of agony. And always, very real, was the terror that Jazzmyn could be placed in the hands of an unsafe guardian.

Doug and Margo felt helpless. There were allegations and interrogations: "How can you two Caucasians raise this African-American child properly? Why didn't you pursue adoption sooner? Do you really love her?" It all took a toll on Margo. Her body absorbed the stress, and she suffered a string of physical symptoms.

Finally, after months of delays, a decision was made. Their adoption of Jazzmyn was legal. They had a party, a time to dedicate Jazzmyn to the Lord and to thank family and friends for all the prayers and support. Jazzmyn, at four years old, was the belle of the ball.

What haunts Doug and Margo are all the other children who don't have strong advocates and are lost. It seems scandalous when love, freely offered, costs the lovers so much. Will the months of agony, the debts, and the suffering surrounding the adoption of Jazzmyn serve as reminders to us of the forgotten children?

> *The things we see now are here today, gone tomorrow. But the things we can't see now will last forever.*
>
> **2 Corinthians 4:18**

I press my nose against the glass of life and strain to see past my own breathy clouds. Maybe what I'm looking for can't be seen. A character in Madeline L'Engle's *A Wrinkle in Time* reminds me that "What can be seen is temporary. What is unseen is eternal." Perhaps clarity isn't my greatest need. Maybe what I need is simply to believe that someone is walking beside me.

I just received a Valentine from five-year-old Jazzmyn. She is announcing the arrival of her new little sister, Mia Isabella. Doug, Margo, and Jazzmyn flew to Guatemala to bring her home. She's almost one. She has bright brown eyes, thick dark hair, and front teeth peeking through. The biggest surprise? Mia's two older siblings, an eleven-year-old boy and an eight-year-old girl also need adoption. Doug and Margo met them on their trip to pick up baby Mia, and they will be the newest members of the family. Neither speaks a word of English yet. Both are excited about belonging to a family and having parents.

When Doug and Margo married, he was certain about one thing: no kids. He and Margo would find other ways to be generous, other avenues for service. They opened their home to Young Life groups, raised money for nonprofits, and led small groups at church. But then Jazzmyn's mother knocked on their door. And Mia's smile captivated their hearts. Their windows were flung open to the sunshine of four beautiful children. And Doug, so certain before, has never seen life more clearly.

 **to ponder**

1. Have you ever been so anxious to see life with clarity that you actually created your own "cloud cover"? What is one thing you are struggling to get clarity on?

2. How have you determined to move forward, doing your best even when you lack clarity? What steps have you taken in faith?

thinking of a key

We think of the key, each in his prison
Thinking of the key.

T. S. Eliot

My uncle Robert once had a license plate on the back of his car that read "No Exit." Now he's gone. I am on a flight to his memorial service, deeply grateful for his life and grappling with what it meant and means.

In seminary, his journey took him away from faith rather than deeper into it. He was a person who personified grace while never embracing it. He was divorced twice, his heart broken after two "pastor's daughters" walked away, yet his love somehow enlarged. Not a man of words, acts of service became his language. When his body was ravaged by Huntington's disease, an ex-wife was among those who provided around-the-clock hospice care.

Uncle Robert looked exactly like the Jesus in all the paintings — shoulder-length wavy brown hair, olive skin, beard, and sandals. He was a professor of artificial intelligence who loved unsolvable mysteries and contradictions. I think he felt safer in a sea of doubt than in the harbor of certainty.

Most people talk a good game, but their lives fall short. Uncle Robert seemed to believe with his body — his mind was the last to know the Spirit in his heart. And then his body shut down long before his mind and he was unable to move or speak. What was it like for a man who spoke with loving actions to lie imprisoned in a failing body?

We have a framed print of Holman Hunt's painting *The Light of the World*. The original hangs in Keble College in Oxford. In it, Christ knocks at a rough door with no handle on the outside, looking for the world just like my uncle Robert looked. Instead of the No Exit of his license plate, I hope he slipped the key into the lock and walked out, exiting this world into paradise.

Uncle Robert's memorial service was held in a garden in downtown Austin, Texas. We sat in the July heat beneath shade trees — his daughters, grandsons, brother and sister-in-law, nieces, nephews, uncles, and friends. I thought of the opening section of T. S. Eliot's *The Waste Land*, called "The Burial of the Dead." It is about asking questions, starting a journey, crossing the threshold. It is about the pain of lost opportunities to love, about the intense suffering of being awakened, about a sort of limbo between good and evil in the "Unreal City."

> *We are closest to God in the darkness, stumbling along blindly.*
> **Madeline L'Engle**

I find myself fantasizing about hosting Eliot and Uncle Robert at a dinner party. Eliot in his dark suit and cane, Robert in his sandals and jeans. When Jesus said it was harder for a rich man to enter the kingdom of heaven than for a camel to go through the eye of a needle, I wonder if he wasn't talking about all types of wealth. Intellectual wealth — brain banks overflowing with capacity and curiosity — might be one type that prevents the humility necessary to reach for redemption. What would Eliot have told Uncle Robert about the leap of faith that both supersedes and celebrates intellectual knowing?

When my thoughts finally ceased, the service was drawing to a close. The only choir was the resounding buzzing of cicadas, rising and falling in rhythm.

As we walked out of the garden, it began to rain.

 **to ponder**

1. Have you ever experienced a greater comfort level with doubt than certainty? How do you hold on to doubt? What are the areas that trouble you most?

2. What type of "wealth" might be preventing you from experiencing the gift of faith?

surface tension

Yet there the nightingale
Filled all the desert with invoidable voice
And still she cried, and still the world pursues.

T. S. Eliot

Water has a skin on its surface where the molecules hold tightly together. It's surprising to discover that water has skin, a surface tension, when it seems so fluid, so penetrable. But things are not always what they seem.

Skin is protection. If someone isn't easily hurt, we say they have "thick skin." Where our skin is tested, we develop calluses that prevent painful blisters. But thick skin can also be a danger when we can no longer feel the texture and the rub of life. The challenge is to maintain just the right level of elasticity in just the right place at just the right time. So often I get it backwards.

My friends George and Arlys Osborne live with their daughter, Hanna, on the edge of downtown Seattle, where established estates blend with newer developments. They have been in an old, elegant home for twenty-five years and have lovingly restored its welcoming wrap-around porch, gracious gardens, fruit trees, and expansive lawn. They host weddings, parties, and celebrations of every kind.

The Osbornes are connected to their neighborhood and generous with their hospitality. Theirs is the opposite of a gated estate. When homeless travelers find shelter under their trees and food from the branches, they are welcomed. When strangers join the gathered family and friends on the Fourth of July to watch the fireworks, they are given a drink and a warm blanket. The back door into the kitchen stands open most of the time, ready to greet visitors.

> *Soak me in your laundry and I'll come out clean, scrub me and I'll have a snow-white life.*
> **Psalm 51**

But in the past several years, a problem has developed. A mentally ill neighbor, obsessed with their daughter, has become an angry stalker. Tolerated at first — "He doesn't know what he's doing" — the Osbornes have had to involve the police. Hanna no longer feels safe in her own home. And now the Osbornes are faced with having to become a gated family. They have been blistered.

And calluses are forming. Nothing is more painful to a father's soul than the threat of danger to his daughter. Arlys is in my small group, and recently we met in her home to pray for protection, for healing, for God's intervention. We prayed that this sick man's family would take ownership and help him, that he would be relocated to a place where he cannot harm Hanna or any other child. We prayed for healing for Hanna, for divine wisdom for the Osbornes. We prayed because calluses are forming on the beautiful, blistered hearts of the Osbornes, the family that embodies gracious openness.

This is our daily struggle with surface tension. Soap weakens the surface tension on water, making it flexible and elastic. I keep thinking of our prayers as an invitation to God to enter our souls with exactly the right amount of soap to break up the tension.

Last night we had a family campfire at our favorite place, Discovery Beach. We gathered driftwood and stoked a roaring fire. When the coals were just right, we pulled out the graham crackers, marshmallows, Hershey bars, and the super-duper rotating extending tongs we bought Les for Father's Day. With some new friends, we toasted marshmallows to perfection (losing some into the flames) and devoured piping hot s'mores.

At home, the boys bathe off the campfire smell. They lounge in the water, covered in bubbles, playing and waiting for me to do the serious scrubbing.

The truth is that we can't do this scrubbing by ourselves. Our souls are created, like drops of water, with a certain amount of surface tension. We pull together; we protect. And it is only God's surfactant spirit who can bring on the bubbles.

I wrote a poem for Hanna on her sixteenth birthday. This beautiful young woman lives a remarkable life. She volunteers at Seattle's Children's Hospital, where she swaddles preemie babies and interprets for bewildered, frightened Spanish-speaking patients; she serves as coxswain on her racing crew; she plays saxophone in a jazz ensemble. Hanna gives so much of herself. She is blown by

> *May the road rise up to meet you,*
> *may the wind be ever at your back.*
> *May the sun shine warm upon your face,*
> *and the rain fall softly on your fields.*
> *And until we meet again, may God*
> *hold you in the hollow of his hand.*
> **Irish Blessing**

God, graceful enough to spin and pirouette in the changing winds. May her blisters soften and heal.

For Hanna

The water I give will be an artesian spring within,
gushing fountains of endless life.

John 4:14

This moment is drenched in beauty
Like your mom's garden at dawn.
It's your time — here, now.
Yet always,
There are those who are dry
Whose moments, days, lifetimes
are deadwood — Ready kindling for fire.
And you'll have thirsty moments too.
Weak, cotton-mouthed, and soul parched.
Never forget,
Your heart is a spring.
Living waters flow in you.
And just the grace of your presence
Brings life all around you.
Never feel small.
Someone has to be
the first drop of rain.

 **to ponder**

1. Have you ever felt like you developed a blister or callous on your soul? Is your tendency, when it comes to life, to be under-protective or overprotective?

2. How have you allowed God to break up the "surface tension" on your soul, bringing more flexibility and health?

stony places

Here is no water but only rock
Rock and no water and the sandy road
The road winding above among the mountains
Which are mountains of rock without water.

T. S. Eliot

My aunt Jill has a small house on a corner lot north of Seattle. Even though she rents, she has poured enough labor and love into the yard for it to become a garden oasis. She has a hammock, a swing, a perfect climbing tree, and flowers galore. Since we live in the city with no yard, my boys love visiting Aunt Jill's, where they've spent countless hours digging in the dirt, climbing the tree, running through the grass, and riding bikes. For us, these simple activities are treats.

One of the projects the boys recently took upon themselves was to uncover a huge rock buried in the dirt at the base of an old stump. Though Jill's yard is full of rocks, there was something wonderful in exposing this particular one and rolling it along to a new resting place. They felt hugely satisfied with their accomplishment.

Jill moved to Seattle to live near my mom, her only sister. My mom has the most severe form of juvenile diabetes, called "brittle" diabetes, which is marked by wildly fluctuating blood sugar levels that are nearly impossible to control. Despite her best efforts, she has "reactions," episodes of unconsciousness, nearly every week. The insulin in her system becomes a hallucinogenic, and Mom enters altered realities. She has been hurt time and again. Calls to 9 – 1 – 1 are frequent. With our demanding travel schedule and two busy little boys, Jill's move from Texas to Seattle to be near Mom felt like God's divine guidance providing a guardian angel.

Jill planned for the transition on sheer faith. She resigned from her church in Austin, said her goodbyes to dear friends and parishioners who grieved her departure, and packed her belongings. Just as she was scheduled to depart, she stumbled on a neighborhood walk and severely injured her knee. Emergency surgery delayed her move. The moving van arrived in Seattle with her boxes while she convalesced in Texas.

With limited mobility following surgery, her planned hospital chaplaincy work was out — too much walking. In the process of seeking employment, it became clear that her vocational calling would not provide immediate work. Ministry positions for women are rare. Job openings for middle-aged women are rarer still. This bright, gifted, credentialed woman found herself stalled, in a ministry wasteland.

> *I love the rain. I want the feeling of it on my face.*
> **Katherine Mansfield**

My aunt Jill has been an immeasurable gift. She pours herself out in generous acts of service for all of us. She cares for our sons, John and Jackson, when our intense speaking schedule takes us away, which is most weeks. She is so vigilant in her care of Mom that 9 –1–1 calls have been reduced to a minimum. And all the while, she has experienced setback after setback in her vocational search.

It is a mystery. Jill stepped out in obedience to God's call and found herself in a spiritual wasteland. She has blessed us, but for her the journey has been dry. She arrived in rainy Seattle from dry Austin only to find a personal and vocational drought.

This brings us to the growing rock pile on the side of Aunt Jill's house. These rocks have meaning, purpose. One by one, these rocks have been placed. After an important encounter with God, or a season of prayer, or a moment of meaning, Jill has taken a rock and placed it there as a memorial. The rocks have been gathered along beaches and from wooded paths. Some are simply picked from her yard. As time has passed and year has layered on year, the pile has grown into "a mountain of rock." There it sits in the midst of her lush, green lawn, a metaphor for her journey through a dry and weary wasteland. It is a holy place. Aunt Jill has arranged those dry rocks into a pile of worship.

 **to ponder**

1. Have you ever stepped out in obedience to God and found yourself in a wasteland? How did you cope with the disappointment?

2. How have you continued to worship and trust God when your life seems to contradict what you believe about God's promises to take care of you?

Quarry

Hard as a rock is
It bows to water
Scrapes to ice
With great force
The frozen water pushes out
Rock crumbles
Tumbles down
Even drops of rain
That splash against a slope
Chisel all within their scope.
Still,
Ocean floor and canyon walls
Gibraltar, Garden of the Gods,
Solid, you defy the odds.
More than that,
Igneous, sedimentary, metamorphic styles,
At a meeting place,
Arranged in piles
Became memorials,
What fossils you contain
What traces,
remnants of our pain.

Sacrificial places.
Geologists can't begin to explain
How ignited,
Metamorphic with God's flame
You conferred
Transformation graces.
But the water
And the blood
Brought on a new age
Gracious flood
Eroded rock
Of sin within.
Make my life a quarry,
Mine for stone
Metal, mineral,
rarest gem,
Whatever can be found
Be used for him.

death by water

He passed the stages of his age and youth
Entering the whirlpool.

T. S. Eliot

Arlys grew up in Africa with missionary parents. One day her parents traveled to an outlying village, and Arlys's mother discovered the red dress she was wearing was causing a stir. Red was the color of evil. So, in her pragmatic spirit, she unzipped her dress and stripped down to her white slip, reasoning that she was still wearing far more modest clothing than any other woman in sight. She worked all day, a relief worker in lingerie. She knew she'd raise an eyebrow or two at the missions board, but that wasn't about to stop her from doing her work.

When Arlys was six, the family joined some friends at a river for a rare vacation. Familiar with the site, her older brother ran ahead, eager to jump into the river's cooling waters. But that day, spring rains had turned the river into a swirling danger zone. Her brother jumped in from a high bank. Arlys, her younger brother, and her parents saw him struggling in the current and calling for help.

Arlys remembers the scene vividly. Her father sprinted to the river's edge, her mother trailing behind and pleading, "But you can't swim!"

Her father, before he leaped in, replied, "He's my son! I can do nothing less!"

Father and son drowned together in the river, and Arlys was left standing with her little brother and mother on the riverbank. Alone in Africa.

> *He who was living is now dead*
> *We who were living are now dying*
> *With a little patience.*
>
> **T. S. Eliot**

Arlys's mom struggled alone to care for her two children. Her son was hearing impaired and had special needs. Arlys was only six when she was put on a plane and sent to boarding school. She's been an adult since first grade.

Arlys has the kind of beautiful soul that sometimes emerges from the chrysalis of severe loss. She isn't waiting to die; she's learning to live. This year she signed up for swimming lessons.

 to ponder

1. Have you ever had a loss so severe a part of you had to grow up too soon? How has that shaped who you are?

2. Have you ever attempted to overcome a deep fear and rewrite your life story? What is one thing you could commit to doing that would help you to get unstuck in an area of fear and loss?

feet in the sand

Amongst the rock one cannot stop or think
Sweat is dry and feet are in the sand.

T. S. Eliot

Death Valley averages two inches of rain a year. Now *that* is dry. It also boasts the hottest temperature ever recorded in the United States — 134 degrees. Summer temperatures of 125 degrees are common. And the Atacama Desert in Chile once went for fourteen years without rain. Almost a decade and a half — that's a dry season and *then* some.

Have you ever known someone in a similar place? A drought so long you can hardly believe it's true? Life doesn't flourish in such desert places — it clings on, barely surviving, and often dies.

My son John was a preemie. At birth he weighed a pound and a half and was one foot long. A full-term baby is about five times heavier and more than half a foot longer. A mother can wrap her thumb and middle finger around the leg of her baby; I could place my hand on John's back and touch my fingertips at his belly button. John weighed only a little more than a Venti Frapuccino.

Preemies struggle to eat. To learn to suck, swallow, and breathe is a large task for such a small being. It was almost impossible for John, whose digestive system hadn't formed properly. There was a gap in his intestine that was infected. He was losing weight. After two weeks, John had to undergo surgery.

The surgery was successful. John slowly recovered. He was able to eat, and we slowly began to settle into a routine. From the day John was born, I committed myself to providing breast milk. Preemies need every possible way to strengthen their immune system.

But John was never able to feed naturally. At first he used a tube and then tiny bottles that were smaller than the ones I had used with my baby dolls as a child. He drank two cc's at a time, every two hours. That's about a teaspoonful of milk. This regimen required that I pump all of my milk, every two hours, twenty-four hours a day. I froze and labeled meticulously all the breast milk that I could. I pumped for almost a year before my body rebelled. Hormones are not released by a pump like they are with a baby, and the supply dwindled. There was nothing cozy in this arrangement. I felt as cold as the vials of milk in my freezer.

Many chronic challenges followed. After spending so many months tethered to a ventilator, John developed a hyper gag reflex. It took almost nothing to trigger that reflex, causing him to lose much of what he ate. Preemies are extra sensitive to food textures and tastes, and John's sensitivity was even more extreme than most. Food was threatening, not pleasurable. He refused to eat most things. Those he did try came back up more often than not. The simple task of eating, of taking in nutrients to nurture his little body, became insurmountable. At the age of one, a speech therapist began working with John on feeding issues. More than a year passed with little progress.

At the age of three, John was still being sustained by baby formula designed for infants under one. He couldn't tolerate formulas designed for older kids, even ones designed for kids with food resistance. One day in Nashville, where we were speaking, John was struggling. In desperation I went to a snack stand to ask for hot water to make a bottle of formula. The woman at the stand berated me for having a toddler on a bottle. I was devastated. I also was afraid that John was becoming old enough to feel ashamed.

We discovered a new experimental group program and jumped at the opportunity to participate. Every week we journeyed to Children's Hospital and met with Lynn, our speech therapist, and a small group of young children and their moms who shared many of the same challenges with food that John had.

We played with food, created things with food, tasted food, and processed our reactions. We moms were coached in how to react to our children's choking and gagging. The strategy was to never seem overly concerned. This wasn't easy. Every time John choked on something, I felt that old familiar panic rising within me. It was a relic from John's failure as a preemie to master the suck, swallow, and breathe sequence that caused frequent chokes that triggered alarms in the Neonatal Intensive Care unit that prompted medical teams to give immediate emergency care. It was as if those alarms had been installed within me and the message to my brain was "Emergency!"

The power of peer influence was a great tool for both children and parents. John faced each session with anxiety for twelve weeks. Eating was downright scary. The demands to eat were exceedingly hard for his little "pleaser" personality. The therapist and the treatment were excellent. At the end of the course, Lynn handed out "graduation" certificates to all the children — except John.

John received a carefully framed "invitation" to come back for the next group. Which we did. And the next one after that.

Time passed. John's food aversions continued. He learned to run down the hall to the toilet every time he needed to throw up. He took care of it all by himself without a fuss — the directive from the therapist. Les and I came to see it as a "normal" part of our lives. We have memories of John throwing up in every possible location that you would want to avoid: restaurants with white linen tablecloths, grocery store aisles, church pews, airplanes. Once Les, his clothing badly soiled, had to wear a waiter's uniform home from a local café.

Having a child unable to eat made me doubt myself. I saw his tiny bony frame and my heart felt like it would shatter. I took it personally. My failure lodged deep in my spirit at a place I had never felt an ache before. I woke up every morning to despair.

Looking back, I can't identify when things began to change. They just did. At five years of age, John finally tasted, and swallowed, and digested his first bites of fruit and vegetables and meat. Until then, the only food he had mastered was cheese. Cheese probably saved his life.

John was finally expanding his menu, slowly, haltingly, cautiously, and not without a fight. The chronic physical symptoms had created an emotional fallout in his relationship to food. Eating brought with it new issues. How can we increase his volume? How can we whet his appetite? Bit by bit, things began to change.

John is still a picky eater. Recently John was diagnosed with "failure to thrive" because his body weight isn't on the chart for his age. Tests continue to evaluate his hormone levels. Labs are taken on his digestive system. Doctors remain uncertain of what, if anything, should be done for him.

Every time I see John take a bite of salmon, or spinach, or even lick an ice cream cone, I marvel. It's a miracle. Two miracles, really. We all survived the drought and, somehow, John adapted.

In the desert, after a rainfall, color explodes everywhere. Flowers bloom overnight in response to the rain. They last for only a short time, but they make an appearance. They celebrate.

So do I. Grace before a meal is less a ritual than a time of true celebration. "Give us this day our daily bread." And thank you, *really*, for the ability to eat it.

 **to ponder**

1. Have you ever had a season so dry you awakened every day to a sense of despair?

2. How did you adapt to life in your dry season?

part iii

dew drops

I sat upon the shore
Fishing, with the arid plain behind me.

T. S. Eliot

Dew beautifies. A spider's web, although a wonder of nature, is more often a symbol of neglect and disrepair than of loveliness and a fresh beginning. As dust collects, they become cobwebs, unable to trap wary insects. Yet covered in dew, this symbol is transformed into intricate, shimmering lace. What was a haunting symbol of the passage of time becomes a captivating work of art. Effective spider webs don't call attention to themselves. But when dew forms on a web, it has the opposite effect. Moist drops highlight the brilliance of the web with stunning clarity. They make us see the invisible.

When my friend Larie turned sixty, she decided to throw a party. As a single woman, she had never experienced a wedding, a wedding shower, or a baby shower. In fact, she couldn't remember even one occasion when she had celebrated lavishly with her friends. She decided it was high time.

Larie is a bright, gifted, modest woman. She was dedicated to ministry and has served on mission fields in Japan, in denominational offices, and at Christian colleges. But money is tight. Her physical disability payments don't come close to covering her medical expenses, never mind a bash. But she had a small inheritance and she decided to earmark it as "party money."

When her friends discovered she wanted to throw a party, they asked for the privilege of helping. So, against her protests, a committee was formed and the party began to take on a life of its own. They created invitations, came up with a theme, and the guest list grew. Larie was paying the bill — she was crystal clear on that point — because she wanted her friends to be lavished with love. The party committee created a mock "prom" theme to evoke a sense of youthfulness and fun.

Tables were decorated with fancy cloths and centered with teeming fishbowls (my son Jackson won the newest member of our family, Bluefish Bob, during one of the party games). Food tables lined the walls. During the hilarious program, Larie sang a solo with total commitment, completely off-key. It made us nervous to watch,

> *I have found the paradox that if I love until it hurts, then there is no hurt, but only more love.*
> **Mother Teresa of Calcutta**

which she enjoyed immensely. Finally she was crowned "prom" queen and escorted around the room by a tuxedoed nephew.

The entire evening was fun, funny, and absolutely off the wall — did I mention her name is Larie Wall? Larie, whose disability produces more physical suffering than any one person should have to endure, was filled with joy from the top of her crown to her glittering high-heeled shoes.

She wasn't the only joyful one. The room was full of people blessed from knowing her. We all sensed something, an unexpected goodness. One by one, people began to tell stories about Larie. College students who had been mentored and discipled thanked her. Nieces and nephews who had been adored by her revealed their pet name — "B.A.L.D." — after she had cheekily demanded they call her "Beautiful Aunt Larie Dear." Past coworkers, friends, neighbors … the stories went on and on.

My son Jackson took the mic. He was three. He sang "Zippidee-doo-dah!" It captured the moment, especially when he belted out, "Everything is satisfact-ual!"

And it was. It was fresh and glorious, like drops of dew clinging to the silken strands of a grand web in the growing light of the rising sun.

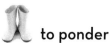 **to ponder**

1. Is there someone or something in your life that is overdue for a celebration?

2. What parts of yourself have been neglected and gone unnoticed for too long? What can you do to remind yourself of the unnoticed beauty in your life?

The Appearing

Glistening beads of water
Appear on blades of green.
The process of your forming
Entirely unseen.
Nights of perfect calm
And clarity
Lead to your refreshing
Charity.
Vapor hovers low
Condenses on the ground.
Cool airs rise
And then,
Rain ascends
from the ground —
Without making a sound.
A miracle of moisture
Upside down.

chapter

sea fog

*The wind
Crosses the brown land, unheard....
And their friends,...
Departed, have left no addresses.*

T. S. Eliot

Sometimes I want to disappear. I long to open my own wardrobe to Narnia or slip on a ring that transports me to the wood between the worlds. I want to be hidden from everyone's gaze. First comes a sense of failure in a relationship, or on a project, or internally, and I begin to look for a way out. I want to hide. I want to regroup.

Fourteen years ago, we adopted a young cat from the Seattle Animal Shelter. Everyone in our family loves Harper. When it comes to tuck-in prayers, Harper is lavished with so many that my aunt declared Harper the most prayed-for cat in the world. Harper always sleeps with John, one paw on him at all times. Jackson, five years younger, is still too wiggly at night to be "safe."

During the daytime, Harper disappears. She is an inventive hider, tucking herself in and under impossibly small nooks. The boys love to report where Harper was found trapped. She clearly loves us and we take tender care of her, but that doesn't stop her from needing to get away from us and be apart. I identify with her yearning to be hidden.

I can be inventive too. Recently my email went down, and rather than seeking to fix the problem, I waited patiently — virtuously — for it to be fixed for months. I wanted to be concerned that it was difficult to contact me, but I wasn't. When I'm hiding, I'm really glad to listen to your sweet phone message, and I intend to let you know how much I appreciate you ... but I won't. When Norah Jones sings soulfully, "I don't know why I didn't come," I think, *amen.* I can be downright rude. It's one of my most unlikable qualities, and it makes me sad to think of what I have missed out on and who I may have hurt.

Like my friend Kate. Her mom died on Easter weekend after a long, brave battle with cancer. Death in the midst of resurrection. Kate, a nurse, provided much of the physical care herself at home rather than sending her mom to hospice. Kate and I have been close since high school — she was a bridesmaid in my wedding and we share so many memories. We haven't lived in the same city for decades, but I still hold her dear in my heart.

When a mutual friend called to say that Kate's mom had died, I intended to call Kate immediately. I cried for her. I thought about her as I went through my day. But then, in the midst of my busyness, I didn't call. That failure, of course, made me feel guilty and even less inclined to call. I can hardly believe I'm still stalling. Kate must think I've forgotten her. She doesn't know I've cried for her, thought of her, prayed for her. I have — but I've kept it hidden.

Some people manage to hide away for good reasons. Jesus regularly had times apart from his disciples and the crowds. He had mountains and gardens he went to for prayer. After Paul had his Damascus Road experience, he went under the radar for a time before he surfaced to begin his missionary work.

These times of withdrawal weren't destructive, although they might have disappointed some. There is something inherently healthy about hiding at the right time, in the right place, for the right reasons. I've started to pray for God's Spirit to be like a fog in my life — for the Spirit to descend and cover me when it is time for me to be hidden. And to equip me with the courage I need to remain fully present and non-anxious until he gives me the gift of retreat.

The beach is my place apart. I imagine myself on the edge of the sea, surrounded by a holy fog and the soft, insistent voice of the only One I need to hear. If you ever stumble upon me there, don't be surprised if I look a little disappointed to be found.

 **to ponder**

1. Are there times you feel the urge to withdraw from life and hide away? What triggers this need for you?

2. Are there times you have chosen to withdraw as a form of escape? Are you able to allow yourself time that you set apart as a healthy choice? How do you know the difference?

Be Still

Rain falls,
Snow drifts,
Sleet and hail
Descend —
hard
and crisp.
But when water stops,
And floats in the air,
Touching the earth,
With delicate care,
And is denser
than a hazy mist —
Fog has arrived.
For me,
This is bliss.
The best kind of fog
Hangs over the sea
And wraps its blanket
Over earth
And Tree.
And the magic of it is
To disappear —
And still to be.

19

chapter

globes of ice

The boat responded
Gaily, to the hand expert with sail and oar
The sea was calm, your heart would have responded
Gaily, when invited, beating obedient
To controlling hands.

T. S. Eliot

In 1970, the year my family moved to Kansas from Texas, there was such a bad storm in Coffeyville that a hailstone fell to the ground measuring a bit over seventeen inches around. That's a piece of ice as big as a cantaloupe. Even normal hail can damage property, people, and animals. Hail falls at a speed of more than twenty miles an hour. Storm winds intensify its punch.

My friend Debbie told me about a couple caught in the middle of a hailstorm of life. The new youth pastor at her church has a baby boy named Joncee, who was born with a rare genetically inherited cancer in his eye. His parents understood what might happen and prepared themselves for radiation therapy or, at worst, an artificial eye. When an X-ray detected fast-growing tumors, an operation to remove the eye was scheduled.

As doctors prepped little Joncee for this dramatic surgery, they found his blood counts were off. Either infection was ravaging his body or he had leukemia. Next came bone marrow tests. His parents were weak with fear.

They knew there was a storm coming, but not *this* kind of storm. Not *these* hailstones. A sense of overwhelming paralysis comes with such intimate pain. The morning of the test, Debbie took the young family to Starbucks. It was all she could think to do for the young couple as they awoke to the day that could change their lives.

The apostle Peter speaks confidently of a day that is coming when we'll have it all — life healed and whole. "I know how great this makes you feel," he says, "even though you have to put up with every kind of aggravation in the meantime" (1 Peter 1:6).

Every part of me believes this. Needs to believe it. But it's that "in the meantime" bit that wraps around my heart like an icy vice. How do you live — how do you order a coffee — when you're taking your baby to the hospital?

Peter pleads with us to "call out to God for help" and to believe that "he helps — he's a good Father that way" (1 Peter 1:6).

And so I do. I call out for little Joncee and for his mom and dad. I do it because the prayers of strangers and friends of friends changed my life when my own baby needed heaven's hand.

I was once told that all the Christians in a certain prison, under the ministry of a friend, were bonded in prayer for my John. Something about those toughened men praying for a tiny boy they had never met worked its way into my soul.

> *The quality of mercy is not strained;*
> *It droppeth as the gentle rain from heaven*
> *Upon the place beneath. It is twice blessed:*
> *It blesseth him that gives, and him that takes.*
> **William Shakespeare**

Even now, I set that memory on the table in moments when I feel alone. But still I sit, raw with grief, and try not to shake in fear and anger and ache.

Peter understood the struggle. Jesus asked him over and over, for reasons known only to Jesus and perhaps to Peter, "Do you love me?"

Dumbfounded, Peter finally said, "Master, you know everything there is to know. You've *got* to know that I love you."

Jesus tells Peter that his life will end in great suffering. "So follow me."

Peter flails. He's trying to make sense — or make peace. He wants to know what's going to happen to his friend John.

Jesus doesn't indulge him. "If I want him to live until I come again, what's that to you?" (John 21:22).

This is a moment of absolute clarity.

This same Peter is the one who later, in hard-won wisdom, says, "Your life is a journey you must travel with a deep consciousness of God." I listen when Peter talks. He knows what it's like to meet Christ, to talk with him on the beach beside a crackling fire, to tear into piping hot fish prepared by his friend and Savior. How much Peter must have loved that bright morning.

Peter seems to understand what it's like to be me. He says, "You never saw him, yet you love him. You still don't see him, yet you trust him — with laughter and singing. Because you kept on believing, you'll get what you're looking forward to: total salvation" (1 Peter 1:8 – 9).

Life healed and whole.

But still. In the meantime.

How in God's name are we to live through storms like these? How are we to live in God's name?

Debbie has a special connection to Joncee. After a freak accident, Debbie has had a constant struggle with sight. Despite multiple surgeries, she has continuing eye problems — chronic pain, dizziness, infections, partial loss of sight. Her body can tolerate the medicine that dulls her pain for only two more months. She has no idea what is next or how the story will end.

No one does. I have a quote tacked on my bulletin board. Gilda Radner, the comedian who battled cancer and ultimately lost, said, "Some stories don't have a clear beginning, middle, and end. Life is about not knowing, having to change, taking the moment and making the best of it, without knowing what's going to happen next. Delicious ambiguity."

I want to find the ambiguity delicious. I know it can be. Each of us is called to be part of a story whose end is life — healed and whole.

But still.

Today the hailstones are as big as cantaloupes, and clouds stretch across the horizon. Help your children, Father. Save us.

 **to ponder**

1. Are there stormy situations in your life that are causing you to live in the meantime? If so, what are they?

2. How have you coped with the ambiguity of seemingly unanswered prayers or prolonged suffering?

Pelted

Frozen raindrops
And whirling winds
Make globes of ice
That fall and spin
Between the Black and
Caspian Seas —
Over Great Plains,
And now,
On me.
You pelt me,
And I run for cover.
It feels like you've been spurned
By an unresponsive lover.
And I,
The innocent passerby,
Am left here,
With you,
An angry sky.

20

chapter

little raindrops

In a flash of lightning. Then a damp gust
Bringing rain.

T. S. Eliot

Today the chestnut tree outside Anne Frank's attic window will be cut down. The tree, which sprouted a century and a half ago, has been badly damaged by fungus and moths. On February 23, 1944, Anne wrote this in her journal:

> From my favorite spot on the floor I look up at the blue sky and the bare chestnut tree, on whose branches little raindrops shine, appearing like silver, and at the sea gulls and other birds as they glide on the wind. As long as this exists, and I may live to see it, this sunshine, the cloudless skies — while this lasts I cannot be unhappy. (*The Diary of a Young Girl*, 1952)

Anne, confined for over two years in her indoor hiding place, died of typhus at the Bergen-Belsen concentration camp one year later.

Seattle is covered in chestnut trees, their bare branches reach to the gray sky and drip with silvery drops of rain. I gaze out my window at the double of Anne's symbol of happiness and reach unsuccessfully for that response inside myself. I am reminded instead of Shakespeare's "boughs which shake against the cold, / Bare ruin'd choirs, where late the sweet birds sang" in his seventy-third sonnet.

It is Thanksgiving week. Even amid bare branches, I know that I have cause to celebrate their fruit. During our morning commute, my boys and I take on the task of naming things we are thankful for that begin with each letter of the alphabet in succession. We begin our list with airplanes that take us on adventures, balloons in the shape of pirate swords, chocolate everything, Douglas (a school friend), elephants — we can't think of a really good answer for "E" this early in the morning — and then we get to "F."

John, my third grader, says "Freedom," and I'm impressed in the easy way mothers are with the insights of our own children. I'm also a bit ashamed; I was thinking of "feathers." John explains to his little brother that in some places, people aren't allowed to worship God, that they have to hide scraps of paper with Bible verses on them just to learn about him. Jackson is stunned and intrigued. Secrets and sneaking and super-secret spy activities are popular pastimes for John and Jackson.

I thought of the patronizing glances and nervous interactions I had with a group of people recently after being transparent about my faith. Seattle is a pretty secular city, but my thoughts weren't about the attitudes of my companions — they were about me, about how disappointed I was that my hands began to tremble ever so slightly. About how anxiety corrupted my clarity, making me less articulate than I really am. About how I felt small and scared.

Stealth is great if you're a kid playing a game of super-secret spies. But stealth in the midst of freedom feels like anti-gratitude. God may be a stealthy God, working quietly behind the scenes in unseen and subtle ways. Jesus was constantly commanding people he healed not to tell anyone what had happened. God's not in the PR business.

But God's people? I'm not sure God asks *me*, anywhere, to be self-protective, tentative, socially savvy.

Anne Frank stayed hidden for the most serious reason imaginable —to stay alive. Confined, lacking all freedom, she looked for happiness in something as small as a drop of rain, silvered by the sky and clinging to a bare chestnut branch.

That's the kind of smallness I want. Not a small voice, but a choice to see the small, shimmering clues of God's presence that are all around me. This is work requiring total attention, ignoring the forest to see each tree as a testament. While this lasts, I cannot be unhappy.

 to ponder

1. Have you ever been in a situation where you felt yourself allowing your voice to be small out of fear? What do you need to allow yourself to say, even if you might feel afraid?

2. When have you experienced deep gratitude by attending mindfully to even the small blessings in your life? What is one specific thing you feel thankful for now?

ice dream

Winter kept us warm, covering
Earth in forgetful snow.

T. S. Eliot

It is December first and it is snowing. The timing is perfect. It feels like the opposite of the light that turns red just when you need it to be green or the phone that stops ringing just when you finally find it.

In this perfectly timed moment, the flakes are huge and magical, a swirling show, falling like confetti at a parade. These flakes are collections of dozens and even hundreds of snow crystals clinging together, each flake nearly an inch wide. From the seventeenth floor, we can watch the snow as it falls with our downward view that creates a floating sensation. We giggle with delight.

This snow is nothing like the artificial snow we made earlier in the week for our gingerbread houses. Tired of the old standby — coconut — we purchased packets of "snow in a bowl." Mixing a powdery concoction with water, we did indeed create something snow-like that we sprinkled on our gingerbread houses, only to discover the next day that it had melted our candy cane trees and turned our snow pink.

Seattle doesn't get much snow. Most winters we are graced with only one or two storms. With the exception of our Olympic and Cascade mountain ranges — Mt. Rainer earned the US record for the most snowfall in one year in 1971 when over a thousand inches fell — we're more of a rain state. But it's nice to look outside the city and see our mountains wearing dress whites all winter long, taking your breath away like a loved one in a white tuxedo (whether four or forty-four).

Tonight the snow falls on a slant, and something about the angle triggers an association for me. Earlier in the day I'd been to a special program with my mom, a performance of the Shorecrest Dance Troupe, a gaggle of angular, adorable adolescent girls in Scottish kilts and argyle. They enthusiastically introduced their dance as the "Taking off the Pants Dance," a true celebration of liberation by men who had been forbidden to wear their kilts under oppressive English rule and were again free to be their Scottish selves.

I watch the snow falling, huge flakes spinning and slanting down into the darkness, and think of it as a dance. In Seattle, snow is liberating. Life grinds to a halt. A city ill-equipped for such storms has no choice but to shut down its productivity, as if voters and taxpayers have conspired to leave Seattle without resources. We raise our snow-white flag of surrender. Why not? Snow days are wonderful fun.

Snow is also an important source of water for us; those mountain melts are crucial through the summer. Snow is also an important source of insulation, creating a protective layer between the cold winter air and hibernating animals and even plants. Snow forms a literal blanket. Like a wonderful throw blanket at the end of the bed to use while indulging in a power nap, this powdery snow fluffs itself over wildlife. It acts as a kind of throw for me too.

The trouble with a forced break is choosing how to use it. Should I fold the laundry? Work on my overdue paper? Read the passages I set aside this morning for my nonexistent quiet time?

Make cookies with the boys? Return phone calls so overdue I feel almost as rude making them as not?

Like the city, I shut down. Paralysis. And before I've chosen how to use my snow time, the large, spiraling flakes begin to fall faster and faster as the snow turns to rain.

The snow melts and life resumes. Canceled plans loom again. I can feel the machine gearing up. My "kilt" is traded for "pants." I turn my face to the wet sky and the falling sleety rain and sing out, "As long as you love me so, Let it snow! Let it snow! Let it snow!"

The only response is silence and rain. It's the kind of silence my son John gives me when he's upset with a disciplinary intervention. It's a bit sulky, but I know he doesn't mean it down deep. So I change my words — "as long as he loves me so."

That's the only insulation I need. I feel quietly liberated. I also feel cold, and wet, and behind on all my urgent to-do's.

But somehow I'm able to resist. I'm able to simply stand, letting *life* be what's important for now. For once I don't need a snow day to slow down and see.

 **to ponder**

1. When have you experienced that gift of a "forced" break in your routine? What did you let go of? What did you do?

2. What is one area of your life that is *important* that has been squeezed out by what is *urgent*? How can you find a way to tend to it?

Circus of White

Shivery, shimmery
Sparkling, soaring, sliding
Star-studded circus of white,
Performing feats of angle and light.
Heaven forms a tently top
Convening the biggest show
On earth.
Dazzled Spectators
Suddenly find
They've nowhere else to go.
Daring Clouds
Perform one final act,
Snow Slows
To a translucent
Stop.
Ice dream dissolves,
Except
In my inner resolve.

thunderhead

There is not even silence in the mountains
But dry sterile thunder without rain.

T. S. Eliot

Surrounding me in Starbucks are neat shelves loaded with bags of Kenyan coffees described as "bright, citrusy, and exotic in flavor." Africa has been on my mind because of the headlines, not coffee roasts. In this warm, cheerful shop, I can close my eyes and see mobs brandishing machetes, bloody victims, and refugees huddled in broken buses with only tea and bread for sustenance.

My son Jackson came home from preschool yesterday proudly adorned with a handcrafted African drum necklace and a simple over-the-shoulder bag sewn from bright African fabric — gifts from his teacher who just returned from studying children's dance in Guinea, West Africa. Her love for the Guinean culture has established a partnership between these preschoolers in Seattle and those in Africa. Jackson's classmates learned several authentic dances and performed them for an audience that responded by giving several thousand dollars to fund educational needs in small villages in Guinea.

This morning, as we moms were partaking in the goodbye rituals of preschool drop-off time, one soulful and intuitive mom connected with this teacher about her "re-entry" process. We commiserated with the shock of returning to the States and how meaningless our Pottery Barn lives seem. The teacher responded that her best moments back home are right at the preschool, in the circle of the children whose singing and community life remind her of the African culture she loves.

As she described this connection between the circle of children here in Seattle and the ones in Africa, I found myself thinking about the body of Christ in Seattle. It is a truly countercultural gathering centered on community, singing, and joy. I wondered if my church could be considered exotic rather than eccentric by my fellow Seattleites. Christianity is a hard pill for this part of the country to swallow. Only 3 percent of my fellow Seattleites are church-going believers. Maybe in the land of Starbucks and Bluetooth headsets, our ability to be "citrusy and exotic" is akin to what Jesus meant by "salt and light" (Matthew 5:13 – 16).

My friend Marta surprised her friends by moving to Nairobi. She's adopted three children and serves at Daystar University, a sister school to Seattle Pacific University where I teach. While I sip a triple tall skinny latte, I think about her in Kenya. I wonder how Jackson's love of world dance, and Marta's life of service, and even the familiar aromas of Starbucks can guide me to a deeper love of my neighbors in Kenya and Seattle.

I long to be an aroma for those here in my neighborhood in need of joyful, singing community. Will people I meet detect a hint of a Person and a place far away, something true and good and relevant to our here and now?

 **to ponder**

1. In what ways do you live a "countercultural" life as a Christian in your world?

2. How might you share a sense of the "citrusy and exotic" or "salt and light" with those whose lives touch yours?

storm chaser

The awful daring of a moment's surrender.
T. S. Eliot

All powerful storms, like thunderstorms, hurricanes, and torna-does, share something in common — air. Such storms are gener-ated when warm air rises, creating an updraft that leads to various outcomes, depending on the presence of water and other envi-ronmental factors. Understanding the conditions that give rise to these storms is the key to preparing for their devastating effects.

One of my husband's favorite gadgets sits in his closet with a continual report on the current temperature and a forecast for the day and week ahead. This guides Les as he chooses his clothing for the day. He feels prepared and in control.

But those gadgets just don't do it for me. I'm more interested in my mood than the weather report. Besides, most mornings I'm too focused on getting the boys up and out the door to listen to the news. My decision-making style is what my husband terms "field independent" — in other words, rather than focusing on my external environment, I focus internally on factors independent of my surroundings.

This can lead to some disastrous clothing choices, like the time I hopped on an airplane with Les and flew from Seattle to Minnesota in my backless mules. Navigating the blizzard in Minneapolis in nearly bare feet was, shall we say, less than pleasant.

People who are seriously tuned in to the weather fascinate me. Some of these people — so-called storm chasers — are so intensely interested in storms that their idea of a good time is getting as close to deadly, twisting winds as possible. Storm chasers get close to study and measure the winds and to photograph the weather formations. They are fascinated with weather warnings, telltale clouds, and barometric pressure. They have an irrepressible need to *experience* the storms.

One storm chaser told me about when she was a child and a tornado touched down in her neighborhood. That close encounter created her deep and abiding fascination with storms, a sort of primal curiosity that was continually pushing her to the next storm site.

While I never intend to become a storm chaser — or even pay much attention to the weather — I have a deep admiration for the courage and curiosity that energize storm chasers. If I'm really honest, the sort of storms that I wish I *could* be more mindful of are the inner storms. Even though I'm focused on my mood here and now, I rarely forecast my future weather.

Inner storms frighten me. Sometimes my emotions gather gale-force speeds so quickly that I feel devastated and shocked. Recently my oldest son had the flu. Now ten years old, he came to me as a pound-and-a-half preemie. Those painfully small footprints left a lasting wound of fear and anxiety in my soul. As his flu-infected frame was bent over a toilet seat retching, I was focused on rubbing his back and bringing any form of comfort and relief that my mother's touch could provide. I was mothering with all my soul.

My husband came to help and quickly noticed we hadn't gotten the seat up (do boys *ever* remember this for *any* reason?). In a firm and loud voice, to be heard over the chaos, he asked John to raise it. This request was well-grounded in reason — who wants to clean more vomit-caked surfaces than they have to?

When John didn't respond, I got defensive for him. Conflict swelled like a thunderhead. Above our poor son's retching frame, the storm quickly grew in force. It became so intense I had to leave the room. The storm lasted well into the evening, draining energy that we needed to care for John.

Seemingly from nowhere, emotional winds had dredged up a collection of relational issues real and imagined, true and exaggerated. Clear skies clouded instantly, leaving me clueless and cold.

What kind of weather report can prepare you for such storms? In the aftermath, with the landscape of my life littered with emotional debris, I wrote a poem.

Meteorologist

Sometimes
I feel so complex
I need a map
Just to orient
To myself
(I've never been good at geography).
And Now
When I feel broadsided
By a thunderhead,
I regret
That I have left unstudied
Parts of me
Prone
To stormy weather
(Like the Great Plains states of
Kansas, Oklahoma, Texas)
I tend to dwell
in the stable
territories
Where I feel safe.

I'd love to have a meteorologist
Dedicated to making
Studied predictions
About me.
To wake up to the very local
Daily weather report
To help me prepare for torrents
Of tears,
Or days like this one
With out-of-the-blue
Thunderheads.
Then I could take care—
Dress in emotional and spiritual
Layers.
But today
I feel vulnerable
Spiritually under-dressed
Seeking shelter
Praying for protection
From me.

 **to ponder**

1. Have you ever been caught off guard by an emotional storm within you? Afterward, were you able to understand your own "weather conditions"?

2. What do you do to tune in to the weather of your soul? What specific signs have you learned to heed as warnings?

low visibility

I can connect
Nothing with nothing.
T. S. Eliot

Many days are overcast. Fog and heavy precipitation make the tops of the trees in the park across the street look like black islands in an undulating sea of gray.

Pushed inside by the chill, I found myself browsing in a little shop called Clover House, a boutique as adorable as it sounds. Amid the trendy gourmet olive oils and funky handmade jewelry and clever cards made of upscale papers, a sea horse of white porcelain caught my eye. It was clean and simple and it captivated me. In a moment of self-indulgence, I bought it. As I pressed the small package deep into my pocket, I thought, I want to collect sea horses. Never in all my life had I ever so much as *considered* such a collection. Yet as suddenly as it had occurred to me, I knew that it was exactly what I should do.

The sea is a place of deep delight for me. I am at home on the beach in every circumstance and season. The sea horse, this paradoxical and mysterious creature, sums it all up. Madeline L'Engle said, "That's the way things come clear. All of a sudden. And then you realize how obvious they've been all along" (*The Arm of the Starfish*, 1965). Like a fog lifting to reveal a scene previously hidden, I felt somehow more whole, like a part of me that I hadn't yet known or enjoyed had been discovered.

It reminds me of the Johari windowpane model of the self that I taught to my students at Seattle Pacific University. It takes the terrain of the soul and divides it into fourths, each quarter based on a single dynamic reality of being known.

There are places within us that are familiar and that we freely share with others. This is the "open self." It might be our sense of style or humor or personality quirks. The better the friend, the deeper the "open" places go. It feels good to know little quirky things about the people we love, like their standing order at Starbucks or that they tend to run about ten minutes late. It feels even better to know what makes them weep or their most embarrassing moment. Yet no matter how deep the layers of knowing go, there is more that remains hidden.

The second pane is the part of us that is known to us but that we don't share with others. This is the "hidden self." All of us have hidden thoughts, feelings, memories, choices. Shame and fear cause us to dig holes and bury dark moments in the camouflage of our personal terrain. What is hidden can be forgotten, but it is never gone. We dig up such hidden thoughts in moments of solitude; then, looking over our shoulder, we cover them up again.

This is a place where grace operates. There is a kind of spiritual archaeology that God seems to be actively involved in, reverently, with brush and pick. The more we allow God's knowing of us to come into our awareness, the more we risk and the more deeply we are known by others, and the more hope there is for healing. Secrets are draining. The joy and liveliness of our personal presence is diminished when we are distracted by the work of hiding.

Once in third grade I shared a poem that I loved. It was actually lyrics to a children's song called "Can I Borrow Your Burro?" from a record album called *Dr. Fun House*. When the class erupted in laughter and the teacher responded with words of affirmation, I suddenly realized that they assumed I wrote the poem. Too embarrassed — and too pleased — I neglected to clear up this misperception. My teacher asked me for my copy of the lyrics, which I had written from memory on a piece of notebook paper. I tried to brush off the twinge of guilt I felt.

A few weeks later, the principal officiously entered the room and called me to the front of the class. My teacher, Mrs. Williams, had a *big* surprise for me, announced the principal. She had secretly entered my poem in a children's poetry contest and it had won the first-place trophy, which was now held in the hands of the smiling principal! Stunned and overwhelmed with guilt, I fled the room and hid in the girl's restroom.

Mrs. Williams found me curled up on the floor of a stall, sobbing. After a frank talk, we left together. She had me keep my trophy as "a monumental reminder of the importance of telling the truth." I had to carry that huge golden trophy home with me later that day. I quickly hid it under my bed, hoping to avoid a certain awkward conversation with my mom.

She discovered my hidden trophy while making my bed the next morning and, thinking I was being modest, she took it out and displayed it on my dresser. I came home to her wide smile and praise. How could I disappoint her? Once again — and so soon! — I took the self-protective path of hiddenness and chose not to tell the truth. But by that night, my secret had drained my soul and I burst into a torrent of tears and confessed.

All I remember is sleeping through the night for the first time in ages. Secrets are difficult. They divide our focus, distract us from the present, and distance us from the people we would love to know and be known by.

There are also parts of us that are hidden — not *by* us, but *from* us. This is the "blind self." There is much within us that is known by others but not by us. Perhaps it is a part of ourselves we would rather disown, or a part of our self we can't yet see. It may be complex or even beautiful; it might astonish us to recognize it. When the people in our lives speak truthfully to us about what they see, we find ourselves expanding, deepening, and broadening, like someone has thrown open a window to our soul.

A wise counselor said to me, "Leslie, when you talk about things that are deeply troubling to you, maybe even overwhelming or crushing to your spirit, things you feel might break you unless you get support, you say you are hurting, but you say it in such a way that you actually send the message, 'I'm OK. I've got a handle on this. I'm fundamentally fine here.' So the words you're *saying* don't sink in. They don't seem real. Consequently, the people who love you fail to offer support because you present yourself as put together. It is confusing, almost paradoxical. We don't know which message is the truth, but we tend to trust your nonverbal message more than your words. And the nonverbal sends the message, 'I don't really need you; I'm just letting you know how I am.'"

I was in a therapy session at the time. There had been a robbery in a little deli across the street from the therapist's office. Someone had been injured in the struggle, and I had stumbled onto the scene in the immediate aftermath. It had distressed me deeply. Everything about how I conveyed this moment to my counselor became a laboratory for her to address a pattern in me that I was oblivious to. No sooner had the words been spoken than they accomplished their intended purpose.

When something is true, you know it.

And when you know it, you can't believe you didn't see it before. All of a sudden you realize how obvious it was all along. I was literally preventing myself from receiving the support I wanted. A part of me that had been known to *others* was finally known to *me* — a part that was crucial to my ability to love and be loved.

The fourth and final pane in the Johari window belongs to that mysterious part of our self that is unknown to us and unknown to others. This is the "unknown self." For Christians, this is the part of us known only to God, perhaps the part that will be revealed only when we finally meet God face to face and become our truest self, our best self, a more full reflection of God's own self.

When this moment comes — when every tear is wiped away by the light of the Light — we will feel a sense of "of courseness" about it somehow. But for now it remains utterly unknown.

I imagine myself atop a sea horse, drawn forward through the deep water in wonder and expectation. Yet some places are murky and clouded. I breathe a simple prayer for the faith to trust God with all that remains hidden and undiscovered within me until the moment it appears in the Light.

 to ponder

1. Have you ever had a flash of insight that came suddenly and you then realized a part of you had known this all along? What was it that became clear to you?

2. When have you experienced feedback that revealed your "blind self" to you? How did you react to this insight?

Grace like Rain

There are few things more lovely
Than the scent of a spring rain
Delicate, earthy, clean
Forgiveness comes close
That astonishing moment
When you see yourself
Through the eyes of another
Rimmed in translucent circles
Of Grace
And discover
The ripple effects
Like a baptismal sprinkling
Have left
Even the darkest soiled ground
Of your soul
As capable of growth
As the rain leaves
A patch of dirt

scent of rain

By the waters of Leman I sat down and wept...
Sweet Thames, run softly till I end my song,
Sweet Thames, run softly, for I speak not loud or long.

T. S. Eliot

Spring rain smells fresh not in *spite* of its earthy, dirt-tinged scent but *because* of it. It's that perfect paradoxical mixture — the freshest, crispest, cleanest scent intermingled with that unmistakable ancient and earthy smell that hints at the history contained in soil: plant and animal decay, organic material fertilized with all manner of dead and living things. Ancient and fresh — the scent of a spring rain is like smelling the entire life cycle in a momentary whiff of air.

Smells have a supernatural ability. No matter our age, a particular smell has the ability to take us back to our childhood in an instant, transporting us through time and space back to a vivid moment of personal history that has been buried in our soil of memory for decades. Most of our stored memories are from experiences we've had between the years of fifteen and thirty. But for reasons not completely understood by scientists, olfactory senses trigger memories of an earlier stage, between the age of five and ten. In part, this is because the ability to smell is housed in the "emotional brain" and seems to work like a sort of index key for our most primitive memories.

We all have triggers — for me the smell of fresh, hot glazed donuts transports me in an instant to the back roads of Texas where my family once stopped at a mom-and-pop donut shop on the outskirts of Garner State Park. We were all loaded too close together in one car, laughing and enjoying the sunshine and anticipating a float trip down the Frio River. I already felt lighter than air when in through the rolled-down car windows wafted the smell of sugary sweetness and dough and hot oil. It was heady. There was instant agreement that we should pull over and cram down as many of those melt-in-your-mouth treats as we could.

The smell of orange juice takes me back in time, but not to a happy place. My mom has had severe juvenile diabetes all my life. Her blood sugars are more erratic than 99 percent of the diabetic population. Consequently, she can and does slide into a diabetic coma. When I was two and home alone with my mom, it happened again. It was a Sunday, after church, and my mom was stretched out on the living room sofa, still in her Sunday dress. I couldn't wake her. My father, a pastor who would normally be home on Sunday, was away on a trip. So I went into action. I dragged a chair over to the refrigerator to reach the orange juice on the top shelf and poured a glass for her to drink. I knew from watching my dad that orange juice helped Mom when she was having a problem. What I didn't know was that when Mom was unconscious, she couldn't swallow. The orange juice dribbled down her chin and stained her best Sunday dress.

Now I was scared and worried that I had ruined her dress. I sat there smelling the pungent, acidic scent of that spilled juice and wondering what to do. I decided to call for help. My parents had already taught me how to dial "0" to ask the operator for help. The phone was a rotary, so dialing "0" meant pulling it all the way around the circle with my index finger. Dragging that circle seemed to take forever and required all my strength. I was relieved when the operator answered.

But when I asked for help, in what was a very young and hard-to-understand voice, the operator scolded me for playing on the phone and hung up. I was devastated. I went back to my mom, curled up at her feet, and sobbed. I had done all I knew how to do, and I had failed. I was terrified. I eventually fell asleep. I woke up to the sounds of my dad and a medical worker reviving my mom.

To this day, I don't like orange juice. My husband relishes a glass of orange juice every morning, but I avoid it — totally. Reliving such childhood pain and fragility isn't a good way to start the day.

The memory of a particular smell as a trigger may be one of the reasons incense was built into the priestly duties involved in worship for the people of Israel. The incense gave off a unique scent, a mixture of five spices that was never to be used for any other purpose. God understood that the uniquely wonderful fragrance would call his people back to memories of worship and trust. Scent can be a powerful reminder of God's grace, an anchor in our souls for forgiveness and mercy.

Spring rain is a kind of heavenly incense that calls me back to moments of sheer grace — encounters with a holy God whose purity mingles with the organic materials of my body and soul, decay and death mixed with heaven and resurrection. It is a scent as ancient as sin and as fresh as grace.

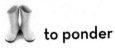 **to ponder**

1. When have you been transported by a smell that triggered a vivid early memory? Do you have any emotional reactions to a particular scent, either positive or negative?

2. What is it that serves as a reminder for you of God's grace?

expectancy

In the mountains, there you feel free.

T. S. Eliot

"I wake expectant," says Annie Dillard, "hoping to learn a new thing" (*The Writing Life*, 1989).

To wake expectant is to open your eyes to the mystery of what might happen. I want to live like that. What I find instead, all too often, is that I wake with *expectations* instead of expectancy. Spoken or unspoken, the expectations I carry with me into each day reduce my ability to live in joyful expectancy. I have expectations of myself, not to mention the long list of expectations I hold for my husband and children.

Sometimes the hardest days of all are those special days of celebration that I have burdened with expectations I haven't even fully admitted to myself. It is difficult for people in our lives to perform the roles we cast for them. Even when they try to play the part of our characters, it drains the authenticity from their words and actions until the effect is almost farcical.

Perhaps that is why some of the best moments in life happen on the most ordinary days — those unselfconscious moments that catch our expectations off guard and invade our beings with the adventure of expectancy. Sometimes our best moments even happen in the graveyard of dashed hopes, the wasteland of unfulfilled expectations, after we've surrendered all our preconceived expectations.

One of the grandest days of my life happened in just such a way. My husband Les and I took a road trip from Seattle to Banff National Park in the Canadian province of Alberta. Life had been so busy, and graduate school, jobs, and family crises had exhausted us. We needed a true vacation.

Within minutes of leaving Seattle, we entered a soothing mountainous wilderness. The drive through western Washington captivated us. Then we crossed into Canada. Something about a border crossing formalizes the mental distance you feel from the dragging demands of ordinary life. Hour after hour, with our attention focused on the landscapes of the Canadian wilderness — soaring mountains, clear gurgling rivers, and massive retiring moose — we began to feel like true adventurers.

We had tried to anticipate our pace and made a few overnight reservations, but one evening at sunset we arrived at the little hamlet of Lake Louise, nestled in the heart of Banff National Park, with nowhere to stay. The lake and mountains were scarcely visible in the dark, but our eyes were drawn to the spectacular beauty of the Chateau at Lake Louise, a lovely old castle-like hotel perfectly placed at lake's edge. This glacial lake is surrounded by snow-capped peaks that evoke images of the Swiss Alps.

Without a reservation, we approached the front desk. They were full. We looked at each other, knowing it meant spending the night in the car without blankets or supplies in the chill mountain air.

We did secure a reservation in the Chateau's restaurant, a cozily appointed cafe with wood-paneled walls called the Walliser Stube. The menu of cheese, meat, and chocolate fondue seemed perfect for the occasion.

We tried to convince ourselves that a warm meal would sustain us through a cold night. We lingered until the lamps were being dimmed by staff eager to get home. It was nearly midnight. We were trying to be brave about spending the night sleeping fitfully and frostily on bucket seats in a parking lot.

> *Sunshine is delicious, rain is refreshing, wind braces up, snow is exhilarating; there is no such thing as bad weather, only different kinds of good weather.*
>
> **John Ruskin**

On impulse, Les decided to check with the front desk one last time before we headed out to our car. The clerk smiled and told us he could offer us the finest room in the hotel — for the price of a regular room. We were filled with gratitude — and looking forward to quilts! As he handed us the keys to the Presidential Suite, he told us our room had a deck that would be ideal for the night's meteor shower, commonly known as "the night of a thousand falling stars." He encouraged us to check in speedily, since the light show was about to start.

I'm the person who always looks up at the black sky just seconds *after* someone else sees a shooting star. The prospect of viewing an actual meteor shower was exciting. Tucked away far from city lights, and at a high altitude, Lake Louise offers a night sky with a rich black canvas. We hurried to the room, grabbed quilts and blankets, and opened the deck door.

We saw first one streak of light, then another, as the meteors began to sail across the sky. Les and I sat side by side, at first pointing out each arc of streaking gold and squealing with delight. Eventually we watched in reverent awe as literally hundreds of meteors with glowing tails blazed across the sky. That night is one of the peak experiences of my life and, in a way Les and I can never quite express in words, one of the most intimate. Only the two of us will ever know the deep mystery and surpassing beauty of that night. It felt like extravagant love and generosity was being lavished on us. Our cups were full and overflowing.

We slept that night like infants. It was the most glorious contentment I can remember this side of childhood.

Rain of Stars

The black night
Seemed dull
And long—
Not just that,
But also wrong.
Then came the rain
Of stars
That silenced me with
Awe.
Like a shepherd
Hearing a choir of angels
Or a wise man
Sighting the Christmas star
It moved me—
Out of failed plans
And into your transcendent
Hands.

Early the next morning, I awoke to what seemed like the sound-track to my dreams. Throwing open the deck doors, I was astonished by the sight of Lake Louise in the early morning light. The glacial water had an other-worldly appearance of milky blue green singular in its purity and vibrancy. Snow-capped mountains formed a clear reflection. I was stunned.

My eyes finally focused on the source of the melody. There stood a man, bathed in the light of dawn, clothed in lederhosen and blowing a twenty-foot Alphorn. These are the horns traditionally used by Swiss mountain dwellers in those pastoral communities so characteristic of the rural Alps. The pure harmonic sound of that larger-than-life instrument was ringing out "Amazing Grace." The music was literally reverberating off the mountains and filling our valley with the most enchanting sounds I had ever heard. It forever changed my vision of heaven.

That experience happened on the heels of imperfect planning, disappointment, and unfulfilled expectations. It filled me with a greater desire to live in a state of *expectancy* — to believe that every moment of the day and night ahead, no matter how divergent from my expectations, will be crammed with the presence and purposes of my loving God.

My expectations *diminish* the possibilities of my life — but my sense of expectancy expands them. At any moment, I may find myself immersed in something just as grand and beyond my comprehension and orchestration as that front-row seat for a rain of stars.

 **to ponder**

1. When have your expectations led to a deep sense of disappointment? What relationships or events seem to trigger high expectations for you?

2. When have you experienced the joy of expectancy, an event or relationship free of any preconceived expectations that turned out to be wonderful?

timing is everything

I rush out as I am and walk the street/with my hair down, so.
What shall we do to-morrow?/ What shall we ever do?

T. S. Eliot

Matthew tells the story of when Jesus was in conversation with some Pharisees and Sadducees. They were pressing Jesus to prove himself; they were looking for a way to reveal how preposterous it was that he claimed to be the son of God. Jesus, quoting this ancient saying, scolded them, saying, "You find it easy enough to forecast the weather — why can't you read the signs of the times?" He was angry, and he "turned on his heel and walked away" (Matthew 16:3 – 4).

It has long been common practice to read the sky to anticipate the weather. With the kind of intuition that comes from experience, much can be discerned from subtle hints. The colors of the sky at sunrise and sunset indicate the kind of weather moving toward us. During sunrise and sunset, the sun is low in the sky, and light is transmitted through the thickest part of the atmosphere, causing a red color which comes from moisture particles and dust suspended in the air. Thus, a red sky at night hints at stable, high-pressure air moving toward the west — basically good weather. A red sky in the morning may reveal a rain storm system moving east because of lower air pressure. For people whose livelihood depended on the weather, studying the heavens for clues was a necessary discipline.

Jesus addresses those whose livelihood depended on studying the heavens in a slightly different way. He is angry because they are asking for something more than what they see in him. This Messiah, God's son, is revealing the vivid colors of a delightful kingdom, yet the Pharisees and Sadducees are asking for something more. Jesus says, "An evil and wanton generation is always wanting signs and wonders" (verse 4).

Spiritual discernment, or even the awareness that springs from keen human observation, has never been my gift. I can count the moments of deep spiritual discernment in my life on one hand. One of those moments five years ago led to the formation of a small group of women.

> *How often have I lain beneath rain on a strange roof, thinking of home.*
> **William Faulkner**

I felt called by God to begin a group that came to be called "Friday Friends." This group of seven women, whose ages and stages span more than two decades, has been an amazing experience. We have laughed and cried and engaged in some of the most expansive conversations and intimate moments I have ever shared. We have felt, collectively, God's activity in our midst. We feel a kind of reverence for the way God put together such an unlikely, unsuspecting collection of women for what seem to be his purposes.

One by one, each of us has been engaged in major personal transitions. My friend Joy recently relocated to Washington, D.C., with her husband, Jim, and their youngest child. Jim was recently hired away from his role with the Seattle Seahawks as quarterback coach and installed as head coach of the Washington Redskins. Joy's life has moved to a level of high visibility that the rest of us marvel at — dinners with ambassadors and celebrities, civic responsibilities, and symbolic events demanding her presence, even as she attempts to homeschool her son and maintain a grounded family life.

In a strange and wonderful symmetry, my friend Sandy also moved to Washington, D.C., at almost exactly the same time as Joy. They have kept the rest of us entertained with stories of getting lost at the Pentagon while trying to find Costco.

Tami, the youngest member of our group and the third transition-maker from our dwindling group of seven women, recently moved with her husband and young sons to Colorado. Family and dear friends, along with the natural beauty of that place, wooed them. The timing was unexpected, but when the opportunity presented itself, they felt the nudge and acted.

Each one of these dear friends had been actively seeking God's purpose and direction in the midst of transition. The process has heightened my own level of awareness. I have joined with them in prayers for discernment and wisdom as we read the heavens while resisting the temptation to ask for signs and wonders.

The transitions of these dear friends have created ripple effects in my life. A group that I've treasured has come to a place of closure. How should I respond to this? What weather is coming? I am studying the heavens these days, straining against my natural obliviousness.

I told Tami that Seattle feels emptier now. I used to live and move with the awareness that this was a city full to overflowing with a network of friends who would halt their lives at a moment's notice to take a call from me, mobilize in a crisis, or drop in unexpectedly for a rich conversation. It's amazing how social a group of seven women can be. Now we are linked by email and cell phones and reunion gatherings, but the weather is shifting, and I'm trying hard to read the forecast.

What does God want me to do with the space in my soul opened by these transitions? What is God calling for now?

I know this: While I pray with my eyes closed and hands folded,

I don't want to miss the revealed presence and purpose of God that already fills the heavens above me.

 **to ponder**

1. Have you experienced a time of deep spiritual discernment in your life? What specifically did you sense God revealing to you?

2. Are there areas in your life now where you feel a lack of clarity or discernment? What are you seeking to better understand?

sprinkled grass

And dry grass singing.
T. S. Eliot

Just before Moses died, while the people of Israel were on the precipice of their Promised Land, God instructed Moses to copy down a song and help the people learn it by heart. Learning by heart requires, above all, repetition. If you've ever caught yourself singing the ABC song while reaching for the order of a letter, you don't need to be convinced that music reaches into the recesses of our being. Singing, like smelling, sets God's goodness deep into our hearts.

Just before graduating from preschool, my five-year-old son Jackson successfully learned a Japanese version of "Head, Shoulders, Knees, and Toes" that is now his favorite party trick. He delights in the enthusiastic applause and words of praise that make his eyes shine, and is fairly indiscriminate about his audience.

Once a song is successfully committed to our long-term memory, with the slightest trigger it has a way of slipping in and out of our conscious mind (I often sing in Japanese while exercising or doing laundry). It becomes a part of the fiber of our being.

Which is why God says to Moses, "This song will be ... a witness to who they are" (Deuteronomy 31:19 – 21). God knew well that the

Israelites would grow comfortable in the land flowing with milk and honey and they would abandon the God who gifted them with it. God told Moses the song would serve as a witness to them about "what went wrong" when things fell apart. Deuteronomy records the words of this incredible song — God's story told as the Song of Moses. It framed a relationship and told a truth so deep that God wanted it not just to be heard, not just to be understood, not just to be known and familiar, but to be learned by heart, contained deep and mysteriously in the recesses of the people's hearts and minds and souls for generations to come.

> *Every experience is a paradox in that it means to be absolute, and yet is relative, in that it somehow always goes beyond itself and yet never escapes itself.*
>
> **T. S. Eliot**

After calling on the heavens to "listen" and requesting the earth's "attention," the song begins, "My teaching, let it fall like a gentle *rain*, my words arrive like morning dew, Like a sprinkling rain on new grass, like spring showers on the garden." The song goes on to say, "God himself took charge of his people, ... He found him out in the wilderness, in an empty, windswept *wasteland*. He threw his arms around him, lavished attention on him, guarding him as the apple of his eye." Finally, the song asks, "Do you see it now? Do you see that I'm the one? Do you see that there's no other god beside me? I bring death and I give life, I wound and I heal — there is no getting away from or around me! I raise my hand in solemn oath; I say, 'I'm always around'" (Deuteronomy 32:39).

I am stunned as I begin to read the imagery of the wasteland and the rain. I think back to a conversation Moses had with God, recounted in Exodus at the beginning of this journey toward the Promised Land, a journey that would span decades and break Moses so deeply that he would be allowed to see the Promised

Land only from a distance. The conversation takes place in a tent called the "Tent of Meeting," set apart from the camp. It was a place where any seeker of God could go.

The Bible tells us that when Moses walked toward the tent, all of the men of Israel, one by one, would take their position at the entrance to their own tents and stand respectfully with their eyes on him until he had entered the Tent of Meeting. At first, the image is of soldiers standing at attention for their commander passing by. But as the story unfolds, we begin to see that the men are waiting for the Pillar of Cloud that would hover over the tent, signaling the presence of God. At this the men would bow low in worship, in unison, each at the threshold of their own tent. It was here, the Bible says, that God "spoke with Moses face-to-face, as neighbors speak to one another" (Exodus 33:11).

In one of these conversations, Moses says, "Look, you tell me, 'Lead this people,' but you don't let me know whom you're going to send with me. You tell me, 'I know you well and you are special to me.' If I am so special to you, let me in on your plans. That way, I will continue being special to you. Don't forget, this is *your* people, your responsibility.'"

God's response to that is, "My presence will go with you. I'll see the journey to the end" (Exodus 33:12 – 14).

That answer is what those of us who are lost in our own empty windswept wastelands most need to hear, no matter the questions we are asking or the journey we are on.

After the death of Moses, it was to Joshua that God continued to say, "Strength! Courage!... Don't be timid; don't get discouraged. God, your God, is with you every step you take" (Joshua 1:7, 9).

Here we are, making our way through a modern wasteland. A couple I know lost their four-year-old boy to leukemia. Months later, in the doctor's office during a routine prenatal checkup for a surprise pregnancy, they were told the mother may have a cancerous tumor. The young husband is incapable of uttering a single prayer. His anger is so fierce that it is boiling within him.

Those of us who know the family are standing in the gap, hoping somehow to carry him with our prayers across this chasm. We beg for God's presence to be known as rain in this wasteland. We struggle to set the truth deep within our hearts that God promises to "see this journey to the end." The words wind themselves unbidden through our thoughts, surfacing as pools of water within.

 **to ponder**

1. Have you ever prayed like Moses did (or wanted to), "If I'm so special to you, let me in on your plans"? What kind of response did you sense from God?

2. What have you "learned by heart" that has been a point of strength or provided direction or comfort for you in a time of need?

Presence

Moses knelt
Barefoot on the dry ground
Watching the bush
Flicker like a candle
Against the horizon
of his hidden life.
Your presence —
Seeking, Blazing, Holy.
Eventually,
Even his own face
Carried your glow.
Even still,
He had his moments,
His doubts, his fears —
He had to somehow
Know
You promised
Not to go.
I take your promise
To Moses
And make it mine.
Can you make me holy?
Will I ever shine?

part iv

moonbow

In the faint moonlight, the grass singing.
T. S. Eliot

My aunt Jill once witnessed a rainbow in the night sky. She and her closest friend were moving my mother across the country. The trip was rigorous, with poor weather, rental truck breakdowns, and exhausting hours. The appearance of the rainbow in the night sky filled them with a sense of awe and a much needed shot of adrenaline to complete the trip.

Astonished by the sight, they decided to investigate. Was there really such a thing or had they somehow imagined it? Moonbows, or lunar rainbows, are a rare — but very real — occurrence. The necessary conditions are extraordinary. The sky must be *very* dark, the moon must be at its brightest, and it must be hanging unusually low in the sky. Rain must be falling opposite the moon. On exactly such a night, the moonbow became for Aunt Jill a symbol of hope.

I'm thinking about the moonbow because I desperately need hope. Yesterday my dear friend Kathy received the dreaded news — her cancer has returned. This aggressive, small-cell lung cancer has moved into her breast. We wept together over the phone, she in Kansas City and I in Seattle.

Kathy is scared, desperate to live, to see her ten-year-old

daughter become a woman, and to somehow come to terms with God's place in this darkness. This recurrence is after a brutal year and a half of the most aggressive chemo and radiation possible — this is the darkest of dark nights.

I've been praying almost without ceasing ever since. For God's appearing. For the brightness of a full moon. For this beating, blinding cancerous storm to be headed in just the right direction — away from the bright light so that a lunar bow breaks across Kathy's field of vision in such astonishing colors that she cannot help but hope. I pray that in every possible way God's presence will be confirmed to her, that she will be enveloped in God's deepest healing and help.

While lunar rainbows are rare, all rainbows capture our attention. Rainbows aren't possible without rain. Each drop of rain acts as a prism and mirror that refracts sunlight into every color of the spectrum.

I can only wonder at the amazement Noah might have felt. Did the arc of the rainbow — the mirror image of the ark of obedience Noah built — drive home the message of God's provision?

Kathy's ark of obedience is built of chemotherapy and radiation. Would that her flood were only forty days! God of dark and light, send her a sign and a seal of your presence and promise. Make your love visible in the blackest of nights.

 **to ponder**

1. Have you ever received a sign of hope in a very dark time? What was it and how did it impact you?

2. Can you think of a person who may need your prayers or acts of service to provide the hope they need to survive a dark night?

magic moment

By this, and this only, we have existed
Which is not to be found in our obituaries.

T. S. Eliot

Sometimes I feel invisible, like no one sees me. Occasionally, that's a good thing. It gives me space. It's not that I'm being actively ignored or given the cold shoulder. It's just that the demands of life are commanding the full attention of the people closest to me.

Left to myself, these can become moments of creativity. Without the high level of accountability usually built in to married life, for instance, I might walk into the kitchen and start tinkering around, pulling dusty cookbooks off the shelf or inventing my own delicacy. If I end up dumping the finished product down the drain and eating Cheerios for dinner, no one is disrupted.

But sometimes being invisible means being deeply lonely. Since my husband is a writer, I have walked through many such seasons in our marriage. Once a new book project is under way — after the typical stops and starts while he wrestles with the outline, and after the main message crystallizes — he goes into production mode. I have never seen a person who is able to focus with more laser intensity than Les. He sequesters himself in his study, emerging only when a break occurs in his creative flow. These breaks aren't based on the demands of convention like mealtimes and bedtimes. He often writes through the night, falling into bed exhausted but satisfied at about the time my morning alarm is sounding.

Les scarcely realizes how separate our lives become. He is so consumed with his project, so fully engaged by its demands, that his awareness of life around him recedes. The rest of us, still living life as usual, are much more deeply aware of his absence than he is of ours. In the early days of our marriage and his writing career, these times would leave me wounded and lonely.

But I began to understand them as a sort of gift. I began to find in them this wonderful time to set my own course, to meander through life at my own (and my children's) whim and fancy. We could go to the beach and linger until our souls were filled to the brim. Coming home wasn't an interruption in the fun but the perfect thing to do. I began to see beauty and freedom in these stretches and to accept them as a gift to my spirit.

However, there is another element to these writing seasons. When the project is complete, it's almost as if Les returns from a trip abroad or awakens from some kind of coma. He re-engages with vigor. I brace myself for the return of his typical laser intensity, when Les is deeply attentive and energized to get his world in order so he can enjoy life again. The adjustment for the rest of us is a bit jarring. He points out the dust and the clutter and the empty shelves in the pantry and takes on our world like he would a writing deadline. Gone are the lazy beach days when we fly under the radar. We are now in the center of his sights. Eventually, that will be marvelous — deep connection and order is restored. But I have learned to brace myself emotionally for the reentry.

Sometimes we desperately *need* to be noticed, to have the person we love fully attentive and totally engaged. We need someone to pick up on those subtle cues like the strain in our voice or the light flickering in our eyes. We need someone to see that we are anxious or overwhelmed, and don't even have the strength to put this into words. We all have inner insecurities that threaten to consume us, regrets that disable us, and fears about the future that freeze us. In these moments, to be seen is everything. All it takes is a knowing glance, a compassionate touch on the shoulder, a simple word of encouragement left on voicemail.

My friend Debbie lives in Pasadena. Once a week we pray together over our cell phones. For reasons that neither of us fully understands, God seems to spring into action in response to our shared prayers more visibly than either of us has ever experienced when praying alone. We seem to have bold faith with one another that we lack by ourselves. Maybe that's why Jesus tells us to pray together and agree with one another — each of us adding our faith to the faith of our friend.

I'll be in my car, commuting in solitude with tears rolling down my cheeks while I grapple with my own tiredness or my feelings of failure. My cell phone will ring and I'll hear Debbie's voice. "Leslie, God awakened me last night, and I prayed for you at 3:30 a.m. Are you okay?"

Have I mentioned that *every time* we pray, Debbie ends by asking God to "wake us in the night" if the other

> *Tears of joy are like the summer rain drops pierced by sunbeams.*
> **Hosea Ballou**

person might need our prayer for the day ahead? I used to ask, "Debbie, what's wrong with God prompting us during the day, preferably after we've had our morning coffee?" But Debbie is resolved that middle-of-the-night prayer sessions are a grace gift.

Maybe she's right. I know that a mere phone call, timed by the Spirit to coincide with a time of discouragement and anxiety, brings strength and courage. I have been noticed, by God's spirit and by a distant friend. I know that I am not alone.

Noticing isn't everything though, is it? There are those soul-changing moments when someone not only sees us but reflects back to us the beautiful brilliance of who we truly are. It's like the magic moment of dawn, when the colors are spread across the horizon like glorious, glowing wings. The shape of our best self has been seen. We feel that we are stretched across the horizon of someone's vision, that their breath catches as they glimpse our true colors. For a brief passing moment, like a sunrise, our God-created image is dazzling. We know the color will disappear soon, but we need to know that there is someone who fully expects to see that dawn again.

I remember the look on my husband's face when I crossed the finish line of the one and only marathon I ever ran. I was twenty-six years old, living in Los Angeles, and decided to train for the LA Marathon. At the end of the race, the instant I stopped running after 26.2 miles and about a million steps, lactic acid flooded my legs. The pain was sudden and crippling. Les literally had to carry me. My face was beet red, and salty tears were streaming down my cheeks.

When I glanced at Les's face, I saw a look of delight and joy. I had fulfilled a dream. It's a look I will never forget.

After the race, he was almost as sore as I was and hobbled into the Jacuzzi at our little graduate-school apartment complex with me. He had been so tense watching and waiting for me that his muscles were strained. I felt the depth of his connection to me that day in a rare and special way. It is a moment I have hidden in my heart — a magic moment.

 **to ponder**

1. Have you ever relished the freedom of feeling "invisible" for a time? What did that freedom allow you to enjoy?

2. When have you felt the gift of someone who truly "sees" you at your very best and delights in who you are? What was that experience like for you?

the emptiest places

These fragments I have shored against my ruins.

T. S. Eliot

My mom was diagnosed with brittle juvenile diabetes when she was twenty-one. A newly married young woman, just finishing college and on her way to serve on the mission field, this was a devastating diagnosis. People with chronic health issues weren't candidates for missionary service. Her body had deteriorated so much before the diagnosis was finally made that she weighed only eighty-five pounds. Because her body couldn't metabolize her food, she was severely malnourished. With the diagnosis of diabetes came the doctor's instructions not to pursue pregnancy. Mom was cautioned in the severest terms that pregnancy would mean sure deformity or death for the baby and possibly her own death.

At the threshold of adulthood, a time when life is about possibilities and dreams and vision for the future, my mother stood in an emotional graveyard and buried her dreams. All that she had anticipated vanished.

My mom and dad decided together to pursue pastoral ministry in the local church and went off to their denominational seminary in the Midwest. Mom used her degree in education to teach in an inner-city neighborhood school while Dad completed his master's of divinity. They lived in a one-room trailer with a fold-down table and bed and scrimped and saved. My dad then pursued a doctorate at the school of theology at Emory University. Mom again secured a teaching position to fund the high tuition and provide for their living expenses. Dad had to sign an agreement that he would not work during his first year of advanced doctoral studies. He went ahead to Atlanta, moving their small trailer to set up life in a new city.

Mom had been battling a mysterious illness and wasn't well enough to travel. Then came the surprise diagnosis: Mom was pregnant, something they had taken every precaution to prevent. Dad quickly withdrew from the doctoral program and took a pastoral assignment at a little church in Weatherfort, Texas. Their lives were in limbo. The future looked dire. Mom's doctor refused to care for her because her pregnancy went against his recommendations. She endured a pregnancy that made her so severely ill that she gained fewer pounds than I weighed at birth. Mom and Dad didn't set up a nursery or pick out a name — these activities were discouraged as they were both told repeatedly that I wouldn't survive.

> *I will give you a full life in the emptiest of places ... you'll be like a well watered garden, a gurgling spring that never runs dry. You'll use the old rubble ... to rebuild the foundations from your past.*
>
> Isaiah 57

When the time came to deliver, Mom checked in at the hospital for the high-risk Caesarean. It was 1964. Mom was given general anesthesia. She remembers waking up in a hospital room from a groggy sleep and being told that she had a living, lovely (if I do say so myself!) little girl.

I was perfectly healthy and weighed in at over seven pounds. I have the original hospital document from Harris Hospital in Fort Worth, Texas. Under *Name* it simply reads, "Baby Girl Young." The doctors were even more astonished than my parents. The excited nursery workers twisted the blonde curls on the top of my head and tied them with a little pink bow before presenting me for the first time to my mom.

I don't know why so many of my parents' early dreams turned to rubble. But I do know that with God's presence, they went on to experience a rich season in ministry and marriage and even this unexpected gift — a full life in the emptiest of places.

One of the joys of living in downtown Seattle is its proximity to freshwater Lake Union. It is a glacial lake that the Duamish tribe called "little waters." At the foot of the Space Needle, Lake Union is a landing strip for seaplanes and a thoroughfare for pleasure boats on their way to Puget Sound. On the east and west sides, it is lined with floating homes, made famous by the movie *Sleepless in Seattle*.

For Father's Day, our family climbed into two double kayaks (a tricky business requiring exact placement of the paddle to secure the kayak and a limber slide into a small compartment with foot pedals) and paddled our way around these waters. John, age ten, shared my kayak, and Jackson, age five, paddled with his dad. We sometimes had to speed up to get out of harm's way as a seaplane headed toward us.

At the north end of Lake Union, directly across from our apartment, is Gasworks Park. It is a beautiful green lawn surrounding a hideous, imposing industrial relic with large towering rusted ruins that seem like the inner workings of a massive factory that have been exposed to open air. A reclaimed gasification plant from the early 1900s, it was transformed by the community of Seattle, which had the foresight to use the old rubble as a foundation for a beautiful, well-watered garden. Kite hill is bright with happy flashes of color as families run and laugh along its length.

Life — full life — has now come to this formerly broken, empty place. Every time I see Gasworks Park, I am reminded of God's amazing promise of transformation. The park is for me a sacred place, a symbol of God's character written in steel and grass.

There have been plenty of empty places in life for my mom and dad. The day Dad decided to end his marriage after thirty-five years was the emptiest day of Mom's life. When the day came for the unwanted divorce, Mom drove herself to the courthouse in Chicago during a blinding rainstorm. I was living in Seattle and couldn't be there. For reasons she can't fully explain, she had to be there when it happened, to witness this dark hour of her life, to make her heart believe it was real. Dad did not attend.

The years immediately following that day stretched out before her in bleak emptiness. Now, more than fifteen years later, her life is full of grandsons and family and community here in Seattle. Life has sprung up from an empty place.

Naturalist John Muir observed that "storms of every sort ... however mysterious and lawless they may seem, are only harmonious notes in the song of creation." In the emptiness after the storm, in the sudden stillness, we can hear the promise of God.

 to ponder

1. What dreams have you had to bury, leaving you feeling empty?

2. Have you ever "reclaimed" a ruined part of your life and created something fresh and good there? Where have you sensed God's restoration in your life?

Empty Places

My mind reviews my
Losses
Like my son's tongue
Seeks out his recent
Missing tooth.
In a way
This whole life is a mouth full
Of baby teeth.
The permanent ones
Will sprout someday
In our gaping gums
And we'll sink those teeth
Into Eternity
And smile.

air currents

The limp leaves
Waited for rain, while the black clouds
Gathered far distant.

T. S. Eliot

Mystery surrounds us, yet we live with the unexplainable impossibilities until, by some miracle, our attention is seized. Children, more fully present than the rest of us, attend to these miracles more readily and sometimes usher us into sanctuaries of awe.

Jackson invited me today. "Mom, why do clouds float, I mean, since they are full of raindrops?" We stood together, gazing at the clouds. I thought in silence about how water was most certainly heavier than air and marveled at the complexity of his question. Then I marveled at my total lack of curiosity regarding this matter. I had somehow reached midlife without giving a single thought to this circus trick.

Later I discovered to my amazement that clouds float because of the interplay between rising air currents and the force of gravity. Air currents push clouds up at a rate that counteracts the downward pull of gravity. This aerodynamic drag creates the effect of clouds hanging suspended in the sky. Most clouds are actually descending, but at a rate so imperceptibly slow it is invisible to the eye. In addition, the droplets that form clouds are *much* lighter than raindrops — it takes about 15 million cloud droplets to make a single raindrop.

I sat in silence, allowing the science to work its way from my head to my heart. The downward tug of gravity is a reality of the spirit. I thought about the discouragement I was feeling over being miserably inadequate for a friend who was fighting for her life against the ravages of cancer. We had ended a recent phone call with her saying hastily, "I've got to go — I've got to go make a bed."

Hot tears had spilled down my cheeks as I considered that my very presence was something she needed to escape from. I felt like I had offered vinegar instead of water to this parched and thirsty friend trudging through the wasteland. In some technological quirk of symmetry, even my emails to her refused to go through and came bouncing back to me, undeliverable. The force of gravity seemed unstoppable.

I thought about the diffuse moisture of cloud droplets, the sheer density of 15 million piled up to the tipping point in a single drop of rain. Clouds remind me of the bowls of incense described in the book of Revelation as the collected prayers of the saints (5:8). Fifteen million is a big number, but it isn't infinite. My diffuse and invisible prayers began to take on a different meaning for me as I pictured them collecting with the prayers of the followers of Christ throughout the ages until — a small real miracle — the first drop of rain in the wasteland.

Our prayers stream to heaven like currents of air, preceded and blown by God's Spirit, by the *pneuma* of God's breath. I pictured my friend, caught between the pull of gravity and the updraft of the air currents, and I prayed that God's grace would float her as gently as she needed. I prayed that the invisible updraft would become visible. I prayed that the sheer audacity of being sustained by a peace that passes all understanding would capture her full attention.

I picture myself as a friend bold enough to cut a hole in the roof of a house and lower my sick companion to the feet of Jesus. I thank God that the sky really is a sanctuary, for "God's glory is on tour in the skies, God-craft on exhibit across the horizon. Madame Day holds classes every morning, Professor Night lectures each evening. Their words aren't heard, their voices aren't recorded, But their silence fills the earth: unspoken truth is spoken everywhere" (Psalm 19:1 – 4).

I pictured the heavens opening for my friend as the breath of our prayers carry her to Jesus. I thank God for the child who ushered me into the sanctuary of the skies, who helped me reclaim my call to serve boldly and believingly in hiddenness. If each of us is a drop of rain, let us ride the updraft of grace where the wind needs to carry us.

 to ponder

1. What is pulling at you right now, like the downward tug of gravity on your spirit?

2. Do you have "air currents" in place in your life, things that pull you upward, toward grace, counteracting the pull of gravity? If so, what are they? If not, what can you do to establish that kind of support?

brooks that hold the sky

A spring
A pool among the rock.
T. S. Eliot

We just returned from a friend's ranch in Montana. The country was expansive and mountainous. Ridges teemed with wildlife. A mother bear and her cubs wandered close to our lodge, as did a coyote and more rattlesnakes than I cared to lay eyes on (that would be more than none, if you're counting). But nothing about the landscape can compete with the sky. In Montana, the sky is the star of the show. Vast and vigorous, its presence is pervasive and commanding.

One day in Big Sky Country we ventured deep into the acreage of the ranch and discovered an abandoned one-room cabin that had been built more than a hundred years ago. The rusty potbelly stove and tin cooking utensils, covered with a thick layer of grime, looked as if they were waiting expectantly for a hot fire and a can of beans to return them to usefulness. It is always sobering to catch a glimpse of something that has survived neglect, yet remained faithful to itself and its purpose.

The true prize came when we rounded a bend to find the source of a sound we had been tracking — a sparkling brook. For the boys, this was better than striking gold. Bright Montana sunlight danced on the spray as the water carved its indelible mark into the sheer walls of stone rising beside it. The Montana sky, captured in the brook's surface, took on a magical motion as the water babbled along over rocks and fallen logs that added dimension and depth to the sky's canvas.

It was an English physicist, Lord John Rayleigh, who in the late 1800s discovered how it is that the sky generally appears to be blue. Even though sunlight appears to be white, it is actually a combination of many colors. Each of these colors has a different frequency, wavelength, and energy. As light travels, it can be bent, reflected, or scattered, and it is this last option — the scattering of the blue light waves — that produces the effect of the blue sky. Blue light is scattered more easily than most colors because its wavelength is shorter.

> *A feeling of sadness and longing that is not akin to pain, and resembles sorrow only as the mist resembles the rain.*
> **Henry Wadsworth Longfellow**

A body of water, of course, can reflect the blue light of the sky like a mirror. However, everything *in* the water — mud particles, plant life, organic debris — will change the way the light is scattered, thus changing the intensity and hue of the color. This brook, rushing before me, reflected vividly the canvas of the blue Montana sky — a living mirror unclouded by anything. The brook is a living cup to hold the sky, yet the sky doesn't seem to shrink into its brookish container. Rather the brook seems to expand as it takes on the largeness of the sky on its liquid surface.

Rabbi Abraham Joshua Heschel encourages us to be "brooks that hold the sky" (*I Asked for Wonder*, 1983). Here we stood, watching that prophecy fulfilled.

Now it is our turn to become a reflection, to bring out the God-colors of the world on the moving surface of our lives. In certain moments, we can even act as prisms, like single drops of rain joined in a downpour, revealing the spectrum of colors streaming down from heaven.

 **to ponder**

1. What debris are you holding onto that might diminish your ability to be a bright reflection of God's light? How can you allow God's grace to carry that debris downstream?

2. When have you felt the joy of serving as a true reflection of God's light and color for someone? How did it make you feel?

walking on mars

There is always another one walking beside you.

T. S. Eliot

My son John is a real space cadet. For the better part of this first decade of his life, he has dreamed of being an astronaut. He has created numerous space suits out of aluminum foil and kitchen strainers and garden gloves and swimming goggles. His *only* request for Christmas this year was a pair of Moon Boots, a retro platform shoe laced with wide rubber bands that suspend the feet to create the sensation of walking in reduced gravity. His room is decorated with his detailed drawings of astronauts and shuttles and moon landings. Most days, space is the first and last thing he thinks about.

For his tenth birthday, we took John on a trip to NASA's Kennedy Space Center at Cape Canaveral, Florida, where he rode the shuttle simulator and purchased an official NASA space suit which he proudly donned for a third grade biography presentation he gave in the persona of Neil Armstrong. John rattles off the names of astronauts the way other boys do baseball players. He knows every mission and every craft. If there was a *Space Jeopardy*, John would be Ken Jennings.

Our family nights sometimes include watching documentaries or movies that tell the stories of space exploration. Somewhere in this process of validating John's passion, there was a desire ignited within John to build his own space capsule. "Sure," we said, suggesting cardboard and markers and the usual random gadgets that served his past projects so well. But this was something different.

John was visibly troubled as he tried to explain to us that this time he meant a *real* space capsule. Like NASA has. He was devastated when we weren't able to validate *this* dream. His spirit was crushed. We tried to get a toehold on something that would evoke the reality for him, so we ordered a cool tent in the shape of a space shuttle. And while John was polite about it, you could see the light of his dreams flickering lower.

The one spark that seemed to remain found an outlet in his prayer life. Each night, after thanking God for the people he loves and asking God to help those he knows need healing or encouragement, John would close earnestly with this final prayer: "and God, help me to get a rocket any way I can. Amen."

The days rolled busily on, but in the quiet spaces of John's spirit, the ember kept smoldering. Then one day, it reignited. He remembered that the Pacific Science Center had a real space capsule on display. He would simply ask them to sell it to him. Confident that he had *finally* found a solution, he composed a letter to the CEO with just such a request and mailed it, along with a picture of himself in his NASA uniform, explaining how much he loved space and what good care he would take of the space capsule. He and his brother began to discuss how they would position the capsule in the playroom if it came and seemed buoyed in spirit by the mere possibility of it.

The school year ended and John enrolled in a fun summer camp at the Science Center. This allowed him to visit the space capsule frequently and to watch other groups learn about it. On the third day of camp, as John and I were walking home hand in hand, John shocked me by saying, "Mom, I decided today that I don't want the space capsule."

I had no idea what could be behind this sudden and absolute change of heart, so I kept listening. "Today I saw all these kids standing in line to see it, and when they get there, they have so much fun inside. If I bought it and took it home, none of those kids would get to enjoy it. I think it wouldn't be the right thing to do."

"Wow, John," I said, "that is one of the most special things you have ever decided. Let's tell Daddy about it tonight." We walked on peacefully. John had released the capsule dream and his heart was free. On the way up to our apartment, we stopped to check the mailbox. Inside was a letter addressed to John Parrott from the CEO of the Science Center. It was a kind letter, with great suggestions to John about pursuing his dream, but of course contained the news, with regrets, that he could not sell the capsule to John (or anyone else) since there were over a million people each year that loved seeing it. It was a shared treasure.

> *Rain is Grace; rain is the sky condescending to the earth; without rain, there would be no life.*
>
> **John Updike**

John was prepared. The Holy Spirit had gone ahead of this letter, transforming its effects by transforming its recipient at exactly the right time. God had not magically produced the rocket of John's dreams, but he had launched John's dream to a higher orbit.

"I don't think the way you think. The way you work isn't the way I work," our God tells us. "For as the sky soars high above earth, so the way I work surpasses the way you work, and the way I think is beyond the way you think" (Isaiah 55:8 – 9).

John was at peace in a deeper way than I had ever known him to be, even as his dreams of space were, once again, necessarily delayed.

Perhaps John will walk on Mars someday. How can we know what the future holds? So many of the things I pray for feel as impossible as a rocket being delivered to my apartment in downtown

Seattle — and forget about walking on another planet! I am praying for the complete healing of my friend with cancer and asking God to do this "any way he can." I am praying for a free beach house for one week of summer vacation for my prayer partner whose ministry budget can't bear the burden of a family vacation this year. I am praying for things I can't even say out loud.

What I'm trying to learn — what I'm struggling to remember — is that I can trust these outlandish requests to God. He knows the best way to respond, and he will. He will send his Holy Spirit to move and work within each desire. And since my Father knows every star by name in the entire expanse of space, I won't be surprised one bit if there is healing, and beachside rest, and maybe even a vacation to Mars.

 to ponder

1. What dreams or desires have shaped your prayers and petitions?

2. Have you ever had the experience of being transformed in the process of an honest, heartfelt prayer request?

deep waters

The brisk swell Rippled both shores.

T. S. Eliot

Today I was a trial juror. The trial was presided over by a prominent Seattle judge. As he entered the room, black robes flowing, we responded in unison to the command to "all rise," and we took our seats again only at his bidding. The case was a colorful one that included a charge of blackmail at the Pacific Science Center. The atmosphere was hushed and edgy. Each juror weighed the matter. Before the trial, the judge addressed the jury with solemn words of responsibility.

Only these words weren't directed toward us as impartial members of a jury designed to carry out justice but as parents of the children who were taking part in this mock trial. Each of us had a child who was about to serve as an "expert witness" for either the prosecution or the defense.

When the judge addressed the parents, we felt the full weight of his charisma and character. He commended us for allowing our young children to participate. He underscored the importance of these very crucial years in the stockpiling of wisdom in the hearts and souls of our children. To drive his point home, he compared the coming teen years to those tense and inevitable moments experienced in NASA's Mission Control when *Apollo 13* was on the dark side of the moon and there was a total communication blackout for several crucial moments. A small explosion — causing the loss of oxygen, water, and use of the propulsion system — had caused the astronauts and their craft to be adrift in space preceding a dangerous reentry into the earth's atmosphere. With a damaged heat shield and limited resources, Mission Control had to guide these men back to Earth with creative science (including a sock as a filter), guts, and prayer.

> *Knowing what is right is like deep water in the heart; a wise person draws from the well within.*
>
> **Proverbs 20:5**

Anyone who has witnessed footage of these moments, said the judge, is fully aware of the emotional charge of this blackout period — and the sheer joy that accompanied that first sight and sounds of the safe astronauts. As parents we will be waiting at "mission control," eagerly watching to see if all that we have built into our children will make it possible for them to navigate safely back to earth following the space odyssey of adolescence.

As parents, we all want to help our children fill the pools of their soul with deep waters that will serve as a future well of wisdom. When we meet someone who seems to lack wisdom, we rightly describe them as "shallow." Shallow is the opposite of everything we hope for in ourselves and in our children. Shallow won't sustain life in the wilderness, let alone the wasteland.

One of the things I appreciated about Jackson's prekindergarten teachers is the simple ritual with which they began every school day. After coats and boots and lunches have been tucked into each child's cubby and hands have been freshly scrubbed, each child is invited to the table where the teacher is waiting with the "morning mystery." These mysteries range from the simple to the sublime — What do you like about your name? What is your favorite superpower? What do you think it means to have compassion?

As a parent, as soon as I heard the mystery question, I had

an instinctive feeling about what the answer would be. It was all I could do some days to stand quietly and patiently while little Jackson silently and thoughtfully pondered these deep matters for what seemed to me an inordinate amount of time. Over the course of the year, I began to understand something new.

So often I find myself acting as if I am filling up the soul of my children like I fill up a small plastic kiddie pool. With hose in hand, it is my job to pour the water in until it reaches its full capacity. What the morning mystery revealed to me was how much the souls of my children are filled to their capacity not by my chit-chat, but by the Living Waters already within them. My job is less about filling them up myself and more about helping them to dip into those waters already present.

Ten months ago, my father-in-law passed away. He was an amazing man, larger than life; he served as the president of two thriving Christian universities for over twenty years and pastored healthy churches throughout his life. He was bright, gifted, driven, and his zest for life was as unflagging as it was contagious. His motto, inscribed over the doorway to his study, read, "Jesus led me all the way." To those of us who knew him, these words rang out as the truest of testimonies. To my children, he was simply "Papa." And for the several months of demanding illness that led to Papa's death, the children earnestly prayed every night for God to "help Papa get better."

Following Papa's death, I found myself sitting down for our nightly prayers with trepidation. Would my sons find that their seemingly unanswered prayers for Papa's healing would hinder their ability to trust? What would this teach them about God? I wondered how I should coach them theologically and emotionally regarding this turn of events. Then, to my great surprise, I listened as my son Jackson began a new prayer ritual the very day he learned of his papa's death, a ritual that he continues nightly to this day.

"Dear Jesus," he prays, his small hands folded and his eyes scrunched shut, "thank you for letting us get to know Papa for a little while before he went to heaven."

Jackson had drawn from the well within and given to me a cup of cold water to refresh my grief-parched soul. Somehow he knew what was right in that moment, in the depths of his soul — gratitude for the gift of his papa, for the joy of having known him. He also knew, with the certainty of a child, that it was time for Papa to make heaven his home.

This is wisdom. This is knowing what is right. This is what will get Jackson — and me, back at "mission control" with my eyes locked on the monitor — through those silent years on the dark side of the moon. This will see him home.

 to ponder

1. Have you ever felt like someone you love was on "the dark side of the moon" and out of reach for a season? How did you endure during the break in communication?

2. When have you been surprised by the deep wisdom contained within someone you know and love? How has it impacted you?

chapter

living fossils

Shantih shantih shantih [Peace which passes all understanding].

T. S. Eliot

Today was an adventure. My two boys and I piled into our Jeep, collected my mom and aunt, and hopped on a ferry to Whidbey Island. It's become our tradition in recent years to plan one special outing each summer that incorporates just the right amount of adventure with just the right amount of physical exertion for a grandmother with diabetes and a great-aunt with a bum knee. The two women are brimming with life yet burdened by limitations of aging.

Today was loosely planned as a garden tour. Stops were mapped out at Hummingbird Farm, which has been compared to "The Secret Garden" in its English beauty; Lavender Winds Farm, currently alive with scent and hues of deep purple and blue; and my personal favorite, Greenbank Farm, where loganberry grows in all its glory and where we consume ridiculous amounts of pie at Rustic Café.

A day like this makes sense — special family time and shared memories that will become stories we tell around future tables spread with holiday feasts. As it turned out, we also saw two little fawns that hadn't yet lost their spots, and we staged a wonderful treasure hunt for leaf skeletons. Gathering these delicate skeleton leaves — that look for all the world like fairy wings — weaves connections across generational lines.

So do the moments like those in the car when ten-year-old John — whose responsibility it is to hold the map and navigate — reads in the guide, "Half the fun is just getting there" and "If you like a maze, you'll enjoy this." He liked the challenge of following such admittedly hard directions. Conversations leisurely unfold among us. Aunt Jill, John's great-aunt, discusses with him the unusual use of the word *legend* as it relates to maps. I share a rare moment alone with my mom, basking in the sun on the deck of the ferry, the sea breeze blowing salty air in and out of our unhurried conversation about books and friends and even painful family history in a way that seems to mimic the flight of the gulls bobbing in the air around us.

> *The paradox of courage is that a man must be a little careless of his life even in order to keep it.*
> **G. K. Chesterton**

These are all good things. Deeply good. But they are not *really* the purpose of this outing. At the heart of our one-day journey is a more solitary goal — renewal. We each seek, in our own way, much needed moments of pure joy and inspiration, of deep peace and true rest that form the shape of our souls. We long for these moments, but they can never be scripted or assured. And so beneath the surface of our activities, we all are keeping one eye open for these grace notes to float through the melody of our moments.

For Jackson, this moment seemed to come as he skipped the soft paths of a labyrinth, smelling the lavender winds mixed with salty sea air gusting from nearby Puget Sound. For John, it was inland, along the woodland path through the deep forest trails. Aunt Jill heard the melody in the stillness and silence that formed the restful heart of the gardens — she said it was the quietest moment she had experienced in the three years since she moved to Seattle.

For Mom, that moment of joy involved the sight of my crisp white T-shirt covered in chocolate fingerprints from my sons' post-ice-cream-cone hugs.

For me, renewal was the discovery of an unusual towering tree — the Monkey Puzzle Tree. When an Englishman first discovered this most unusual evergreen, a native of the Chilean Andes, he observed its reptilian-like armor — the spiked leathery leaves and the unusual twisting branches — and declared that it would certainly create a puzzle for any monkey who wanted to climb it. Quite accidentally, when he pocketed some nuts that he was unable to identify and planted them after they happened to sprout on his voyage home, the tree was transplanted from South America to Europe and became popular as an ornament in English gardens. Monkeys are not, of course, found in the Chilean Andes, but the name stuck.

And it struck me. I thought about the power of recording spontaneous thoughts, about how often what seems to be a private observation, meaningful only to oneself, may actually serve as a catalyst for shared insight and collective truth and emotional connections. I pictured an English explorer scribbling in his travel journal his impressions of this unique tree — and here I was, observing the same delightful evergreen on yet another continent. Seeing that tree invited me to visit, at least in my mind and heart, the original miraculous encounter.

In a way, that is what I find so amazing about the Gospels. When John says, "The Word became flesh and blood and moved into the neighborhood. We saw the glory with our own eyes, the one-of-a-kind glory, like Father, like Son, generous inside and out, true from start to finish" (John 1:14), it has the unmistakable ring of authenticity to it.

These vivid words complete my own experience. They deepen my understanding of my own encounters with the living God who is light and life. They validate and even expand on my ability to know this amazing God through the life of Christ. Across the pages of time, I meet John, and we worship the same ever-living miracle.

The Monkey Puzzle Tree is a living fossil, the closest known relative of a species of vegetation that was alive millions of years ago. In the stories of the Old and New Testaments, we relive the very personal observations and encounters with God that men and women much like us recorded thousands of years ago. Scripture is our living link to the moments when God revealed himself personally and uniquely in the history of the world he created, loves, and will someday fully redeem.

This is renewal, our minds and hearts transformed. May our spiritual seeds sprout and bear fruit far from home, even in the most unlikely and impossible places. May future generations consider the stories of our doubts and of our discoveries and draw renewal.

For now, I'm going to tuck this leaf skeleton into my ribbon board as a reminder. Of growth. Of death. And of the possibility of new life.

 to ponder

1. Describe your most recent experience of rest and renewal. What made it so refreshing and how did it impact you?

2. After sharing a private insight, have you ever discovered it was something other people could relate to and found helpful? What was it and what kind of a reaction did you receive?

postlude

It's been a quarter of a century since Eliot's *The Waste Land* first captured my imagination. I never would have imagined that the images of his poem would become in so many ways synonymous with the terrain in my own life — and the aching losses of those I love. The young girl from Kansas would marvel at the woman who has grown so connected with the geography and climate of Seattle, the woman who has discovered an unmistakable sense of the sacred gift of God's presence in something as simple as a drop of rain. Rain is a symbol of God's presence no matter what obvious contradictions exist in our present lives.

Today is September 23, 2008, the one-year anniversary of my father-in-law's death. I opened my daily Scripture reading journal this morning to the notes scrawled a year ago today: "Dr. Leslie Parrott Sr. died at 10:39 p.m. at home with Graham. We sat up late, weeping and talking." The strength of attachment we feel to him is just as strong one year later. Our lives are so much fuller for having known him, so much emptier for letting him go.

I think about my aunt Jill, engaged as a chaplain at Bailey Boushay House, a hospice for people living and dying with AIDS and other medical needs. Her ministry demands from her an awareness of God's presence in situations that seem to almost entirely obscure that reality. The pile of rocks beside her home is still growing.

I think about Joncee, whose leukemia is in remission and who is enjoying his life. The weather report is sunny, but neither he nor his parents know what is beyond the horizon.

I think of dear Kathy, who is experiencing the latest round of chemo with the most tender combination of reverent strength and honest doubt that I have ever known.

Like a chapter out of Hebrews, the great cloud of witnesses in my life whose stories shaped my own life parade before me.

The apostle Peter, whose life, like my own, contained the paradoxes of devotion and abandonment, truth and deception, strength and weakness, reminds me that "life is a journey you must travel with a deep consciousness of God" (1 Peter 1:18). My prayer for us in our desert places, however wide and however dry, is that we would hold onto faith until the certain appearing of the first drop of rain.

acknowledgments

Sincere thanks to ...

Angela Scheff. I can't imagine doing this project without you. You embody the perfect editorial paradox of challenge and support — bringing life to words and wisdom to light.

The Zondervan team. The grace you extended as the timeline expanded was unconditional.

Sealy Yates, for the friendship powered with wisdom that guides our work.

My husband, Les. If it weren't for your unwavering belief in me, I wouldn't have written one word. Knowing you, and loving our boys together, is my greatest adventure.

To the friends and family whose stories have defined my life and the pages of this book. You are my window to truth and beauty when life works hard to obscure them both.

To William P. Young for deepening my understanding about the power of living in expectancy in *The Shack*.

To my city, Seattle. You are not just a backdrop for my life journey, but a main character. I love the way you deepen my faith.

Love Talk

Speak Each Other's Language Like You Never Have Before

Drs. Les and Leslie Parrott

A breakthrough discovery in communication for transforming love relationships.

Over and over, couples consistently name "improved communication" as the greatest need in their relationships. *Love Talk*, by acclaimed relationship experts Drs. Les and Leslie Parrott, is a deep yet simple plan full of new insights that will revolutionize communication in love relationships.

In this no-nonsense book, "psychobabble" is translated into easy-to-understand language that clearly teaches you what you need to do — and not do — in order to speak each other's language like you never have before.

Love Talk includes:

- The Love Talk Indicator, a free personalized online assessment (a $30.00 value) to help you determine your unique talk style
- The Secret to Emotional Connection
- Charts and sample conversations
- The most important conversation you'll ever have
- A short course on Communication 101
- Appendix on Practical Help for the "Silent Partner"

Two softcover his and hers workbooks are full of lively exercises and enlightening self-tests that help couples apply what they are learning about communication directly to their relationships.

Hardcover, Jacketed 978-0-310-24596-4

Also Available:

978-0-310-26214-5	Love Talk	Audio CD, Abridged
978-0-310-26467-5	Love Talk Curriculum Kit	DVD
978-0-310-81047-6	Love Talk Starters	Mass Market
978-0-310-26212-1	Love Talk Workbook for Men	Softcover
978-0-310-26213-8	Love Talk Workbook for Women	Softcover

The Parent You Want to Be

Who You Are Matters More Than What You Do

Drs. Les and Leslie Parrott

Being a parent is the most important calling you will ever have – with the emphasis on being. This parenting book is unlike any other: it's a step-by-step guide to selecting and modeling the very traits that you want your child to have. Because, as the authors explain, parenting is more about who you are than what you do.

Children long to be like their parents. That's the secret behind this method of choosing your top traits – your "intentional traits" – and projecting them consistently.

What is the single most important question you can ask yourself as a parent? Find out in this book. You'll also learn the three-step method to avoid becoming the parent you don't want to be … how to hear what your child isn't saying … the single best way to teach a child patience … and much more.

Written in short, designed-for-busy-parent chapters, with self-tests and discussion questions, this book helps you select your top traits and make them stick. Filled with encouragement, inspiring examples, and warm personal stories from their own experiences with their children, this book offers the Parrotts' revolutionary road map to parenting success.

Hardcover, Jacketed 978-0-310-27245-8
Audio CD, Unabridged 978-0-310-27977-8
Audio Download, Unabridged 978-0-310-27978-5

Pick up a copy today at your favorite bookstore!

You Matter More Than You Think

What a Woman Needs to Know about the Difference She Makes

Dr. Leslie Parrott

Am I making a difference?
Does my life matter?

"How can I make a difference when some days I can't even find my keys?" asks award-winning author Leslie Parrott. "I've never been accused of being methodical, orderly, or linear. So when it came to considering my years on this planet, I did so without a sharpened pencil and a pad of paper. Instead, I walked along Discovery Beach, just a few minutes from our home in Seattle.

"Strange, though. All I seemed to ever bring home from my walks on the beach were little pieces of sea glass. Finding these random pieces eventually became a fixation. And, strangely, with each piece I collected, I felt a sense of calm. What could this mean? What was I to discover from this unintentional collection?"

In this poignant and vulnerable book, Leslie shows you how each hodgepodge piece of your life, no matter how haphazard, represents a part of what you do and who you are. While on the surface, none of these pieces may seem to make a terribly dramatic impact, Leslie will show you how they are your life and how when they are collected into a jar — a loving human heart— they become a treasure.

Hardcover, Jacketed 978-0-310-24598-8

Pick up a copy today at your favorite bookstore!

Trading Places

The Best Move You'll Ever Make in Your Marriage

Drs. Les and Leslie Parrott

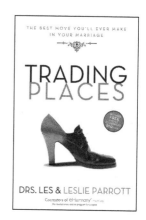

To understand your spouse you've got to walk in his or her shoes.

Ever feel like you're stepping on each other's toes? Then maybe it's time you put yourselves in each other's shoes. Of course that may sound uncomfortable. But it's easier than you think—and it will revolutionize your relationship. In fact, bestselling authors Drs. Les and Leslie Parrott reveal the little-known secrets of putting the time-tested strategy of trading places to work in your own marriage.

In this book, chock-full of practical helps and tips you've never thought of, you'll learn the three-step-strategy to trading places and, as a result, you're sure to:

- Increase your levels of passion
- Bolster your commitment
- Eliminate nagging

- Short-circuit conflict
- Double your laughter
- Forgive more quickly
- Talk more intimately

This book also features a powerful, free online assessment, powered by eHarmony Marriage that instantly improves your inclination to trade places. How? By zeroing in on exactly what you'd most like your spouse to accurately understand about you. In addition, two workbooks with no-nonsense exercises—one for you and one for your spouse—will help you apply each chapter to your own marriage.

Hardcover, Jacketed: 978-0-310-27246-5

Pick up a copy today at your favorite bookstore!

Share Your Thoughts

With the Author: Your comments will be forwarded to the author when you send them to *zauthor@zondervan.com*.

With Zondervan: Submit your review of this book by writing to *zreview@zondervan.com*.

Free Online Resources at
www.zondervan.com

Zondervan AuthorTracker: Be notified whenever your favorite authors publish new books, go on tour, or post an update about what's happening in their lives.

Daily Bible Verses and Devotions: Enrich your life with daily Bible verses or devotions that help you start every morning focused on God.

Free Email Publications: Sign up for newsletters on fiction, Christian living, church ministry, parenting, and more.

Zondervan Bible Search: Find and compare Bible passages in a variety of translations at www.zondervanbiblesearch.com.

Other Benefits: Register yourself to receive online benefits like coupons and special offers, or to participate in research.